HANS WALTER WOLFF

The Old Testament A Guide to Its Writings

translated by Keith R. Crim

London SPCK 1974

First published in Great Britain in 1974
by SPCK
Holy Trinity Church, Marylebone Road
London, NW1 4DU

Reprinted 1979

This book is a translation of *Bibel—Das Alte Testament. Eine Ein-führung in seine Schriften und in die Methoden ihrer Erforschung,* copyright © 1970 by Kreuz-Verlag in Stuttgart, Germany.

Printed in Great Britain by
Lowe & Brydone Printers Limited
Thetford, Norfolk

ISBN 0 281 02780 3

Table of Contents

Introduction: The Old Testament as a Theme of Theology

This book presents the Old Testament Scriptures as a theme of theology, although ancient Israel's collection of pre-Christian writings could also be treated simply as a part of the history of ancient Near Eastern literature. The Old Testament would the more readily be accepted as a theme of Semitic studies if it did not lay claim to any normative value as "the word of God." From the time of Marcion in the second century down to the struggles of faith in our own day, the claim of the Old Testament to make a contribution to theology and to the life of the church has been disputed again and again. Marcion's pupil Apelles rejected the Old Testament as an untrustworthy collection of lies and fables. There were people then who agreed, and there still are. The reader should be aware, therefore, that as he delves into this book he is approaching a theological theme that has been disputed not only as to its details but also as to its basic claim. For many, the Old Testament means a parting of the ways.

This may be the reason that even to the present day study of the Old Testament has lost neither its fascination nor its urgency. Literature of the modern period and even of our current times of upheaval cannot break away from the Old Testament. Negro spirituals such as "Go Down, Moses" and contemporary philosophers such as Ernst Bloch demonstrate even more powerfully than Goethe's *Faust* and Thomas Mann's *Joseph* how Moses and the prophets stir the hopes of oppressed people and arouse them to action. The concerns of the Old Testament reveal themselves as present-day concerns. This in itself may be enough to make the Old Testament a theme of theology.

It certainly was such a theme in the early days of Christianity. Paul taught what faith is by referring to Abraham (Rom. 4; Gal. 3). His great pupil Luke was convinced that Jesus of Nazareth, who had been crucified, could be recognized as the living Lord only with the help of the Old Testament canon (Luke 24:25–32). The parable of the rich man and Lazarus ends in a piece of fundamental counsel. The rich man wants Lazarus to return from the world of the dead in order to witness to his brothers and warn them before it is too late. But Abraham (once again it is the great patriarch who plays the decisive role) rejects as erroneous the idea that a messenger from the dead would be more effective than the words of Scripture: "If they do not hear Moses and the prophets, neither will they be convinced if some one should rise from the dead" (Luke 16:31). The reader of the Gospel of Luke is expected to find in the Old Testament the noblest and best teacher for his life as an informed disciple of Jesus. In similar manner, 2 Tim. 3:15–17 praises the usefulness of Scripture "for teaching, for reproof, for correction, and for training in righteousness, that the man of God may be complete, equipped for every good work."

In the second century the church defended the validity and significance of the Old Testament over against Marcion and the gnostics. Thus Justin and Irenaeus laid down the dictum that the Old Testament was indispensable for the knowledge of

Christ and for a Christian life. There has always been difference of opinion about the relative value of its various themes—law, promise, history—and about the various ways of interpreting them—allegorically, typologically, historically. This is due to the richness of the contents of the various books as well as to the changing nature of the problems faced in succeeding generations. Taken as a whole, however, the canon does not merely answer questions that are brought to it; it actually raises on its own some of the basic themes of theology. Indeed the Old Testament as such would have to be called a major theme of early Christian theology.

Only so can its name in fact be understood. The formal designation "Bible" is as old as the church itself (2 Tim. 4:13 refers to *ta biblia*, "the books") and reflects the unique importance that was accorded it as a matter of course. Only after basic theological reflection was it termed "Old Testament," thereby building on Paul (2 Cor. 3:14) and on Jeremiah (31:31–34). This took place much later, when the New Testament canon was complete. God's old promises are to be distinguished from his newer ones, but not separated from them.

Even the transmission of the Old Testament writings cannot be understood without taking theological motives into account. It was the result of deep crises of faith, as we can see from the oldest instances in which oral traditions took on literary form.

Isaiah is the first to show us how and why prophetic oracles came to be written down. He had threatened Jerusalem with imminent attack by the Assyrians (7:17–20; 8:1–8) and was accordingly accused of being party to a conspiracy (8:12). As a result of this rejection he determines to "bind up the testimony, seal the teachings among my disciples." He says, "I will wait for the Lord, who is hiding his face from the house of Jacob, and I will hope in him" (8:16–17). He writes his words down because they have not yet been fulfilled. The basis, purpose, and goal of writing are made clear by a later word, which he holds fast to as the command of God: "And now, go, write it before them on a tablet, and inscribe it in a book, that it may be for the time to come as a witness for ever. For they are a rebellious people, lying sons, sons who will not hear the instruction of the Lord" (30:8–9). The oracles are written down not to preserve something from the past, but to serve as witnesses to the call that has been issued, witnesses which at a future time will call to account those who have treated it with contempt. Thus the words of the prophets were written down because they had meaning for the future.

A century later, Jeremiah dictated to his friend Baruch oracles that he had spoken over twenty years earlier. Here too the reason for writing the words down is not the respect they had received but the rejection of their testimony. Forbidden to preach in the Temple area, Jeremiah had his words written down in order that the proclamation could be repeated with hope of a better hearing. Even though the prophet is himself prevented from preaching, Baruch can read the scroll and perhaps bring the people to repentance (Jer. 36:1–7).

The history of the canon begins with a warning not to add anything to or take anything away from the word of life that has been proclaimed. This warning is found in the instruction in Deuteronomy (12:32; cf. 4:2), in the command to a prophet (Jer. 26:2), and in the teaching of the wisdom literature (Prov. 30:5–6; Eccles. 3:14). In Revelation, it is extended to words of the New Testament as well (22:18–19). The word must be whole and pure when it reaches the next generation. Why? Those who issue the warning are certain that God's word and attested work remain effective, wholly sufficient for those who will come after them. What they are afraid of is that the promises which encompass the future and this work which will bring in the future could be falsified if something were to be added or taken away.

The completion of the Old Testament canon took place in three major steps. By the end of the fourth century B.C. the Torah with its "five books of Moses"—Genesis, Exodus, Leviticus, Numbers, and Deuteronomy—was complete. We know this because the Samaritans, who broke off relations with Jerusalem at this time, preserved the same text. At the beginning of the second century B.C. Jesus Sirach testified to the completed canon of prophetic books, which included the "later prophets" of Isaiah, Jeremiah, Ezekiel, and the Minor Prophets along with the "earlier prophets" of Joshua, Judges, Samuel, and Kings (Sir. 46:1–49:10). Finally, in the first century A.D. the "Writings" are fixed as the third part of the canon: Psalms, Job, Proverbs, the Five Scrolls (Ruth, Song of Solomon, Ecclesiastes, Lamentations, Esther), Daniel, Chronicles, Ezra, and Nehemiah. In the last decade of the first century A.D. a Jewish synod meeting at Jamnia, eleven miles south of Joppa, rejected speculative apocalypses and syncretistic writings. The canon was limited to the period of revelation from Moses to Ezra (see below, pp. 113 f.).

In Greek "canon" means a straight stick by which something can be supported, aligned, or measured. The corresponding Hebrew word *qaneh* also means "standard." Thus the library of biblical books was brought together as a collection of those writings that set standards and support proper growth. The closing of the canon was in keeping with the inner dynamics whereby the scriptures themselves had come to be written; it involved a recognition of the word that will encounter people in the future, of the writing that is to be read again and again in the expectation that people will heed it and change their lives, of the document that attests the full gift of life from the God of Israel.

This then is how we are to understand the collection as a whole which grew up over the period of a thousand years. At the same time each of the biblical writings, with its distinctive themes and tendencies, is to be regarded as making its own specific contribution to the pointing of the way. Only thus can the significance of the Old Testament as a whole be realized.

This guide to the writings of the Old Testament follows the order of the three major parts of the canon. It first calls attention to the significant materials and then, in connection with representative passages, introduces the reader to the methods of objective research. The improved access which we have today to the riches of the Old Testament writings may help us to see why this book, like no other before or since, has exerted such a tremendous influence on the world of Judaism, Christianity, Islam, and even the most recent phase of atheistic Marxism. Its message alone must demonstrate whether thought and action inspired by the Old Testament can open to all men a new and common path.

1. The Past:
The Historical Books

THE GOD OF ISRAEL: YAHWEH AND THE GODS

The significance of the Old Testament stands or falls with what it says about God. For this reason we must begin with this difficult and decisive theme, or else run the danger of treating subordinate matters in a way that would misrepresent their relative significance. The reader should study the Old Testament itself, and not merely a subjective selection of material. We are looking for the constant element that binds the many themes together.

The Data

No matter how we approach the Torah, the heart of the canon, all its statements center in the name "Yahweh," the name of the God of Israel. From beginning to end the literary framework reveals unmistakably the real subject of all the events. Genesis 1:1 begins, "In the beginning God created the heavens and the earth." The same narrative strand, the "Priestly Document" (see below, pp. 32 ff.), concludes with the observation that under Moses' successor Joshua the Israelites "did as the Lord had commanded Moses" (Deut. 34:9). A postscript, vv. 10–12, explains Yahweh's dealings with Moses: "The Lord knew him face to face" and accomplished through him the work of liberation from Egypt. Thus God's word and work are determinative for all that happens from creation down to the life of Israel under Joshua. This literary framework of the Torah, however, is late in point of time.

If we look for the oldest parts of the Pentateuch, we discover the song of Miriam (Exod. 15:20–21), which the Israelite women sang while they danced and clapped their hands to the point of exhaustion: "Sing to the Lord, for he has triumphed gloriously; the horse and his rider he has thrown into the sea." We can feel the breath of those who have been rescued. They do not sing the power or cunning of the men of Israel, or Moses' skill as leader. Yahweh alone is the one they rejoice in, the one who rescues the oppressed. Modern historical research sees in the song of Miriam the direct response to a historical event in which a group of fugitive Hebrew slaves, their enemies in pursuit of them, were rescued east of the Nile Delta. The song presupposes that the testimony to the God Yahweh was tied directly or indirectly to this event.

The confession that Yahweh led Israel out of Egypt, told in narrative form in the first fifteen chapters of Exodus, forms the nucleus around which the other elements in the Pentateuch traditions crystallized. There also we find Yahweh as the real subject of all the great strands of the tradition. Yahweh led Israel through the desert (Exod. 16–19; Num. 10–21). Yahweh gave Israel the land of Canaan (Num. 13–14). God had earlier promised this land to their ancestors, just as he had promised that the descendants of the patriarchs would become a great nation (Gen. 12–50). All ordering of legal and cultic matters in Israel depends on Yahweh alone, who revealed his will at

Sinai, and not on anything in the life of the people or the nation (Exod. 19–Num. 10). And finally, when the history of Israel, which Yahweh had brought into being, was put into relationship with the traditions of the other nations, which represent the history of all mankind, then here too Yahweh is creator, judge, and sustainer (Gen. 1:1–12:3). So we see that the late framework, the old nucleus, and the various groupings of traditional material exhibit a continuum of statements about God.

What can be said about the Pentateuch is largely true of the rest of the Old Testament as well. The historical accounts from the days of the judges to the time of Ezra vary considerably in their extent, their closeness to the events recounted, and the amount of reflection they exhibit. They may sing Yahweh's direct intervention (Judg. 5), or depict it (Josh. 10:10–14). They may energetically trace the relationships among events and only reluctantly provide a clue to their understanding, as in the account of David's rise at its beginning, "Now the Spirit of the Lord departed from Saul" (1 Sam. 16:14), and at its culmination, "And David became greater and greater, for the Lord, the God of hosts, was with him" (2 Sam. 5:10). They may present for consideration human deeds, ways of conduct, and trials in isolated cases, or in wider contexts as the result of the proclamation of God's word or as a reaction to it (1 Kings 17–19; 2 Kings 17). The theological level is therefore quite varied. Still, no Old Testament presentation of past history keeps us from understanding history in the biblical sense as "the work of Yahweh" (Josh. 24:31; Ps. 44:2; Isa. 5:12). Later historical writing is inconceivable without the influence of classical prophecy. With its formulas for opening oracles, "Thus saith Yahweh," "The word of Yahweh came to me," "Hear the word of Yahweh," Old Testament prophecy counters every attempt to understand it in any other manner than as God speaking.

It goes without saying that the lamentations of Israel, with their characteristic appeal to Yahweh, expect from him alone a change in circumstances, just as the psalms of praise give praise to him alone. Recent research has revealed the international connections of the schools of wisdom literature, a literature which pursues with a single mind worldly phenomena and purely human relationships, but in Israel even the wisdom literature must be seen under the rubric "The fear of the Lord is the beginning of knowledge" (Prov. 1:7; Job 28:28). The Book of Esther is the only biblical book that never mentions God directly, and it refers to him indirectly only once, "from another quarter" (4:14). Its acceptance as canonical was disputed until the last.

These observations merely serve to show that in the Old Testament itself the knowledge of Yahweh, the God of Israel, is an all-pervasive theme of fundamental significance. But does the fact that it speaks everywhere about God make the Old Testament relevant to people for whom gods belong to an outmoded world view?

God and the Gods

This question must come to terms with the fact that in contrast to all other ancient writings the Old Testament never takes God for granted. On the contrary, within the Old Testament there is a lively struggle between Yahweh and the gods which unfolds quite differently from the struggles common within a pantheon. We can anticipate its result and state it here as a thesis: the God to whom the Israelites bore witness stripped the world of its claims to deity, and for all time prevents mankind from deifying the world. This statement does not rest on general and immutable doctrines, because such doctrines are foreign to the Old Testament. It is documented rather by actions and processes in which the liberation of mankind actually takes place and the world is deprived of its claims to divinity. In the Old

Testament there is no tendency to develop a unified theology; the various theologies are articulated on widely separated battle-fronts. Always it is a case of a person being freed from his own gods, and always Yahweh is the one who frees him, through deeds and testimonies.

Let us look at three typical phases of this struggle, which we may refer to as exclusion, subordination, and denial. The decisive factor is Yahweh's claim to exclusiveness, whereby he declares that he is Israel's God "from the time they left Egypt." This is seen in cultic formulas in which Yahweh declares, "I am Yahweh," and at the same time rejects all "other gods" (Exod. 20:2–6; Lev. 19:4; Deut. 4), and in prophetic words such as Hos. 13:4. According to Joshua 24, the covenant with the old Israelite tribes was constituted by a rejection of the gods of their ancestors and of the surrounding nations, coupled with a whole-hearted commitment to Yahweh, who had led their ancestors out of Egypt (Josh. 24:14–28). Exclusion in this sense says nothing whatever about the existence or nonexistence of the other gods. Nor are we to assume that the testimony to Yahweh's exclusive claims was able to effect a general conformity in the variegated religious life of the largely independent clans of Israel.

Indeed, it was precisely because of this diversity that the question of the other gods and how to regard them could not be postponed. The male and female deities of the old native Canaanite population produced fertility in their sacral marriages, and life and death in their battles. They appeared impressive to Israel. This favorable impression is reflected in the criticisms of Hosea and Jeremiah and in the zeal of Elijah against the worship of Baal. Documentation for this struggle is now available as the result of the excavation of texts at Ras Shamra, a ruins in northern Syria. What was Israel to think of the gods of Canaan? Psalm 95:3 praises Yahweh as "a great

King above all gods." In this second phase of the struggle the rejection of the foreign gods took the form of subordinating them to Yahweh. The other gods lost their independent spheres of activity. The only task remaining to them was to honor Yahweh (Ps. 29). Thus exclusion takes the form of subordination. In addition, the subordinated gods can be called to judgment. In Psalm 82 Yahweh accuses the assembled gods of sanctioning oppression. And so he adds, "You shall die like men, and fall like any prince" (v. 7). This total degradation may well be reflected in the frequently used expression "Yahweh of hosts." The word "hosts" can designate the armies of Israel, or the hosts of the stars, or be an abstract plural meaning "power." But the ancient connection of this remarkable name with the "ark of God" (1 Sam. 4:3–4; 2 Sam. 6:2) suggests the possibility that the "hosts" are the divine powers of the surrounding nations. Along with their independent functions their personal names have also been taken away; as those who have been dethroned they serve merely to fill out the realm of the power of "Yahweh of hosts." Instructive pictures of Yahweh's divine court are found in such texts as 1 Kings 22:19–23; Isa. 6:1–7; Job 1:6–12 and 2:1–6. Everywhere the divine beings, including Satan as the heavenly prosecutor, are fully subordinate to Yahweh.

In Psalm 82 the diminution of the power of the other gods takes the form of a sentence of death, and this announces a third phase of the struggle. This third phase finds full expression in the classical prophets, who both rejected and destroyed the gods. Here exclusion means denial. Hosea addressed an Israel that had fallen into worshiping the Canaanite god in the form of an image of a young bull. This worship implied absolute deification of the fertility of cattle and farmland, the epitome of economic power. Hosea says of the image: "A workman made it; it is not God. The calf of Samaria shall be broken in pieces"

(8:6). Isaiah fought against the deification of political and military might (31:3). His contemptuous expression for the idols sounds something like "minigods," and means "bunglers" or "nonentities" (2:8,18). For the gods of the foreign cults Ezekiel coined an insult which today we would have to translate as "shitgods" (6:4,6; 20:7 f.; it appears almost forty times in all). Jeremiah called the gods of Canaan "things that do not profit" (2:8). Second Isaiah (see below, pp. 88, 97 ff.) condemned even the gods of the world power Babylon as "delusion" and "empty wind." They are "nothing" (Isa. 41:24, 29). In this way, economic, political, and religious powers are reduced to their real value—they are only the work of human hands or the product of nature. In Isa. 44:9–20 a song mocks the god who is being worshiped and strips away the illusions about him. The song tells of felling a tree and working the wood. Then it says of the wood, "It becomes fuel for a man; he takes a part of it and warms himself, he kindles a fire and bakes bread; also he makes a god and worships it" (44:15). A daring line of reasoning exposes the god that is the same material as firewood. The first account of creation teaches that even the stars, which in the nations around Israel were worshiped as powers that determined fate, are not to be seen as deities, but as what everyone can observe—as large and small lights, and as helps in fixing the calendar and dividing it into days, months, and years (Gen. 1:14–18). And so the struggles of the Old Testament against the deification of worldly or human powers leads to the possibility of observing all phenomena objectively. That is the presupposition of scientific research, technical civilization, democratic societies, and a peaceful world order. All this is hindered, retarded, and disturbed by old or new deifications of the world, by totalitarian claims of human theories and forces, and not least by the elevation of reason to the position of a mythical king of the gods. Reason's limits, contradictions, and uncertainty about goals are ignored whenever we lose sight of that source of human freedom, that power which strips the world of its claims to deity—the biblical distinction between God and the gods, that is, the knowledge of Yahweh.

Yahweh

Who is Yahweh? We shall see that he is the one who, through his witnesses, makes it not only possible but also necessary to speak responsibly of God in a world that he has stripped of its claims to deity. Only as Yahweh's messengers do his witnesses demythologize the world in such a way that mankind is saved.

How does Yahweh reveal himself? He calls human beings to hear him and to speak for him. What these messengers say determines when and where in the events of history and of nature he is also recognizable. Thus he bound himself to Israel from the time of his promises to the patriarchs and right on through Moses, the mediator. Then prophets of the most diverse types accompanied Israel, brought her down to ruin, but also led her through, gathered her again, and gave her new hope and power. It is no surprise that at the end of this line of messengers stands Jesus of Nazareth, acclaimed as the mediator, the prophet, the Word of God. Yahweh reveals himself in the words of human messengers.

The contents of their messages differ a great deal, depending on the changing social situations and the personality of the various messengers. The more varied the testimony to Yahweh is, the more the variety of the witnesses compels the hearer to pay attention to the particular message that confronts him. Israel's God goes with those whom he addresses as they enter into new and unexpected situations; indeed, he is the one who brings what is new. Although Yahweh thus relates himself to men in varying ways, there are at least three striking things about him, three features which appear constant and clearly distinguish him from the gods of the surrounding nations.

The first is the messengers' constant insistence that Yahweh alone is God. As a concept this was grasped with increasing clarity and had its influence on the editing of older documents. Yahweh never lives in a pantheon. In neighboring cultures, light and darkness, life and death, are gods locked in struggle with each other. In a marriage of the gods the showers of rain awaken the fruitfulness of mother earth. Yahweh is the sovereign Lord over all these polarities; he is the Creator, without any other divine counterpart. It is man, especially the nation Israel, that becomes God's partner. This has far-reaching consequences.

In the second place, Yahweh is not tied to any place. The gods of the surrounding nations are as a rule assigned to geographical locations, weather zones, or specific residences. Yahweh is free to move from place to place. He led his people out of Egypt and through the wilderness; he entered Jerusalem, but he also left it when the people were too sure of him (Ezek. 11:22–23). He is not called after the name of a place or a country, as Melkart is "the Lord of Tyre," or as Baal is connected with Mount Hermon. Above all he is the "God of Israel." Once in the Old Testament he is called the "God of Jerusalem," by an Assyrian who pictured him in terms of the other gods he knew (2 Chron. 32:19). Similarly, in 2 Kings 17:26 ff. he is mistakenly referred to as a "God of the land." But Yahweh is different. It is people, not places, that he saves and judges.

The third distinctive feature is a crucial one. Yahweh cannot and may not be represented in any pictorial form. There is a strict prohibition against making and worshiping any images cast in metal or carved (Exod. 20:4 f.; Lev. 19:4; Deut. 4:15–20). This indicates a distinctive feature of the belief in

Yahweh. And what is this? The surrounding nations made pictures of the solar disk, the thunderbolt, the power of the bull, the generative strength of the male member, the deadly cunning of the snake, the chaos of the raging sea. In this way they analyzed the world through their archaic, mythic science. Yahweh, however, is not to be compared with any of these familiar phenomena of the world, not with "anything that is in heaven above, or that is in the earth beneath, or that is in the water under the earth" (Exod. 20:4). The prohibition of images is the reverse side of the stripping of the world of its deity. Yahweh reveals himself and gives himself to Israel as the sovereign Lord of the demythologized cosmos; his faithfulness is to mankind, not to gods, or places, or world powers. In the Decalogue the prohibition of images is preceded by the statement: "I am the Lord your God, who brought you out of the land of Egypt, out of the house of bondage. You shall have no other gods before me" (Exod. 20:3).

The consequence of this is that Yahweh can be encountered only where he chooses to be present through the reports of his messengers. He is not known through contemplation of the world or through human meditation. He cannot be specified by a picture or by a concept. He comes to us by sending messengers in Israel's turbulent history. For this reason we cannot define him, but only tell about him. "Yahweh" is a name, but in the entire Old Testament an etymological explanation of this name is attempted only once, in Exodus 3, and even more striking than this is the peculiarity of the explanation offered there.

Moses is charged with liberating the Hebrew slaves. He asks the one who gives him this order, "What shall I answer when they want to know your name?" Then God says to Moses, "I am who I am. . . . Say this to the people of Israel, 'I am has sent me to you'" (Exod. 3:14). It sounds, doesn't it, as if God is simply refusing to give his name. Just as images were forbidden, so also the one sending Moses is not to be identified with any known divine being. He can be compared only to himself. Whether this interpretation corresponds to the intention of the author can be seen only by means of a philological explanation of the basic text.

EXCURSUS: *Philology and Exegesis*

The significance of linguistics for exegesis cannot be over-looked here. Exodus 3:14 makes you want to learn Hebrew!

We have translated the Hebrew word *'ehyeh* by "I am" (some translators, following Luther, prefer "I will be"). It would be hard to overlook the similarity of sound between this word and "Yahweh." Hebrew phonology explains why in the name Yahweh the second syllable begins with *w* instead of *y*: dissimilation prevents the unpleasing repetition of the same sound, and the prefix *ya* in the name would have resulted in two *y*'s.

Morphology deals with the meaning of the different prefix. *Ya* changes the first person *'ehyeh* to third person. Out of the self-declaration "I am" we get the confession "He is." This interpretation, however, is disputed. The vocalization of the prefix is certain, on the evidence of the ancient Greek texts that transliterate it, and this form could be taken as a causative ("he brings into being") or as an element in a noun formation ("being," "essence"). This uncertainty strengthens the assumption that the name Yahweh is much older than its explanation in Exod. 3:14.

This is confirmed by comparative philology. Pre-Israelite occurrences of the name can be documented from two Egyptian texts of about 1400 B.C. which mention a "land of Yahweh bedouins." The Egyptian vocalization is only slightly different from the Hebrew. These texts take us to the same general area south of Palestine that is referred to in Exodus 3. This type of name appears to be the shortened form of an old Canaanite name in praise of God: "God continues to reveal himself as the one who helps." So the name is certainly older than the explanation in Exod. 3:14.

An appreciable aid to our understanding comes from semantics. The Hebrew word root *hayah*, which is the basis of *ehyeh* in the explanatory sentence, and probably also the basis of the name Yahweh, means something more dynamic than our auxiliary verb "to be," which is generally used to translate it. It has more of a sense of activity, or revealing oneself. This means that the explanation cannot be taken merely as a refusal to give God's name.

This becomes even clearer when the syntax is considered. Its significance for the explanation of the biblical texts cannot be overestimated. The usual translation, "I am who I am," is questionable, not only because of the meaning of the words but also in reference to the first person pronoun in the relative clause. It is clearly identifiable only in relative clauses that serve as the object of a verb, as Exod. 33:19, "I will be gracious to whom I will be gracious" (cf. Exod. 12:25). It is quite different when the relative clause modifies a preceding subject, for example in Exod. 20:2. Literally the sentence reads, "I am Yahweh, your God, I who have brought you out of Egypt." In English we say more naturally, "I am the Lord your God, who brought you out of the land of Egypt." A similar instance occurs in Lev. 20:24, "I am the Lord your God, who have separated you from the peoples." (The "have" of the Revised Standard Version is an attempt to keep the first person throughout, but we naturally expect "has.")

If we combine the semantic and syntactic observations, we might more accurately translate as, "I reveal myself as the one who reveals himself." Or, "I am (active as) the one who is at work." So the statement refers not only to the uniqueness of

Yahweh but also to his interpretation of himself in his historical activity. This illustration should indicate that philological research is indispensable for biblical studies.

The Only God

This singular and unrepeated explanation of God's name in Exodus 3 confirms the fact that in Israel Yahweh was understood as the one who in sovereign freedom uniquely reveals himself through his deeds in history. We can observe the fierce struggle to establish that he is the sole Lord in Israel; it is seen in the claims to exclusiveness, the subjugation of other gods to Yahweh, and the denial of their reality. In reference to the call of Moses in Exodus 3, there is one additional factor to mention as regards Yahweh's relationship to other gods. In vv. 13–16 Yahweh states that he is the God of Abraham, Isaac, and Jacob. Students of the history of religion see here a secondary identification. With understandable zeal they search for corners of the Old Testament in which the editorial broom of the Deuteronomic purge (see below, pp. 41 f.) may have left undisturbed the names of a few foreign gods alongside the many thousands of occurrences of the name Yahweh. In Genesis we learn of gods of the patriarchs called the "Fear (Relative?) of Isaac" (31:42) and the "Mighty One of Jacob" (49:24). In them Israel could recognize Yahweh because by their very names they were related to the men whom they led and with whom they wandered, and they did not reveal themselves by images but by promises. In other gods as well no contradiction to Yahweh was felt. The El Olam of Gen. 21:33 was the "Everlasting God," and the El Roi of 16:13 was the God who watched over men and women. Such tacit identifications are to be regarded, in terms of the history of religion, as the occupation of new territory. After David's conquest of Jerusalem, the functions of the

Canaanite "highest" God, El Elyon, who was worshiped there, were naturally assumed by Yahweh (Ps. 47:2; cf. 46:4). In such acts of occupation Yahweh's sole lordship was proclaimed. Like the rejection of foreign concepts, so also the absorbing and taking over of the functions of other gods was a step on the road to the insight that Yahweh alone is God and there is none other like unto him.

At the end of the struggle it is possible to say simply "God" instead of "Yahweh." To be sure, we should remember that the name Yahweh is used throughout the Old Testament much more frequently than the word "God." Yahweh occurs sixty-eight hundred times, "Elohim" only a little more than two thousand times. In the "Elohistic" strand in the Pentateuch the name God is used throughout (see below, p. 21); in the Elohistic Psalter (Pss. 42–83; see below, p. 104) it replaces Yahew to a large extent, and in the book of Ecclesiastes it replaces Yahweh completely. And so in the end, Yahweh was victorious over the gods.

Still we should never forget that in the Bible "God" takes the place of a personal name and, as in the case of the Christ event of the New Testament, the historical event takes precedence over the concept. Deuteronomy 12:5 says that the "name" has taken up its habitation in Israel. It is this "name" that calls mankind to be ever vigilant against any deification of that which is purely human and worldly, whereby men would be enslaved by new myths. Testimony to the name Yahweh makes it not only possible but also necessary for men to speak of God in a responsible manner. Whoever shrinks from the use of that name hinders the work of stripping the idols of their power and increases the danger of a renewed confusion of God with the idols, as in the reactionary movement of totalitarian and absolutistic points of view. Old Testament speech about God prepared the way for the kind of theological scholarship which is dedicated to historical and empirical research as over against speculative philosophy. This is because it produced the documents which gave rise to our present world and set goals for our future. In order to see how this is so we must take a closer look at the writings themselves.

BLESSING AND OBEDIENCE: THE YAHWIST AND THE ELOHIST

The research of the past two centuries is in almost total agreement that two older writings constitute the major strands of the Pentateuch. Because these great literary works use different names for God, they are called the "Yahwist" and the "Elohist," respectively. The Yahwist document uses the name Yahweh from the story of creation on, while the Elohist document uses "Elohim" (God)—consistently down to the time of Yahweh's self-revelation in Exodus 3 and for the most part thereafter. Apparently each of these two works at one time brought the major units of traditional material into a literary form. But the written documentation is a relatively late result of a complicated history. Research in the history of the transmission of the material attempts to discover the course followed by the separate blocks of material down to the time when they came together in cycles of stories. A few examples will show how this research works and what its results are.

EXCURSUS: *Tradition History*

An explanation of terms is in order. Tradition history as a method of biblical study regards the formation of literary sources as a decisive turning point in the process of transmission. Thus the history of oral transmission is distinguished from that of literary composition and subsequent editing. The change in methods of transmission calls for a corresponding change in methods of research. The second part of the process, literary transmission, calls for a literary-critical method, which in fact has been practiced now for more than two centuries. It is only in recent decades, however, that the first part of the process, oral transmission, has been studied by methods of the history of tradition in the narrow sense.

Investigation of the preliterary history of the material is altogether necessary, particularly when within one of the literary strands the same material is preserved twice with minor variations, and then appears in similar form in another strand. In Genesis the story of the threat to the ancestral mother is recounted three times, in 12:10–20; 20:1–18; and 26:6–11. The decisive events of the story are the same in all instances and form a completely closed context. The ancestral father finds himself in a foreign land with his wife, who he says is his sister. A danger arises when foreigners wish to have sexual relations with her, but in the nick of time she is recognized as the wife of the stranger and is given back to him. The persons involved in the three texts are different. In Genesis 12 they are Abraham, Sarah, and the Egyptians; in Genesis 20, Abraham, Sarah, and King Abimelech of Gerar; and in Genesis 26, Isaac, Rebecca, and the Philistine king Abimelech. Only one variation in the content is worthy of note—the wife who is said to be her husband's sister comes to be recognized as the ancestral wife in three different ways. In Genesis 12 Pharaoh recognizes that he has done wrong because of the plagues that Yahweh sends on him. In Genesis 20 God reveals the deception to King Abimelech in a dream. And in Genesis 26 the Philistine king looks out a window and sees the husband and wife engaging in intimacies. The well-determined context which the main events have in common forces us to the assumption that the literary variants arose out of what was originally the same material. The differences cannot be explained as due merely to literary activity, however, because two of the accounts belong to the same strand. Genesis 12 and 26 are Yahwistic, and Genesis 20 is Elohistic. We must therefore assume a preliterary history during which the material was handed on.

In Exodus 14–15 the great event of deliverance at the Reed Sea is described in various ways. In one account Moses stretches out his hand so that the waters pile up like walls and Israel is able to pass through, but then the waters flood back over the Egyptians (14:16, 21*a*, 22, 27*a*, 28). Alongside this we hear of an east wind that dried up the sea for Israel, but in such a way that the Egyptian chariots got stuck; Yahweh himself stops them with a glance and throws them into the sea (14:21*b*, 25–26, 27*b*). Moreover, the angel of God and the column of cloud take part in the deliverance; they no longer move on in front of the Israelites but go behind them so that the pursuing Egyptians cannot see their quarry any longer (14:19–20). These individual features are so intermingled in the present writing that probably no effort to disentangle them and assign them to separate literary strands will be able to win general acceptance. In addition, chapter 15 contains poetic accounts of the events, the song of Moses in vv. 1–11 and the song of Miriam in v. 21. Thus Exodus 14–15 shows that in the course of time the events of deliverance at the Reed Sea gave rise to colorful narrations of various sorts in Israel. The written form of these chapters is certainly not the beginning but the end of oral and, in part, written traditions that were full of variants. Nothing of what was proclaimed to the praise of God about Israel's welfare could be allowed to be lost.

It is not only the existence of individual variations in parallel passages that leads us to postulate preliterary transmission. Even in the oldest sources the major blocks of tradition run parallel.

With the exception of the primal history, the Elohist knew of them just as the Yahwist did: stories of the patriarchs, the exodus, the Sinai traditions, the wilderness period, and the occupation of the land. Observation of these broad thematic similarities served in yet another way to advance studies in the history of transmission. Attention was drawn to liturgical texts which contained the themes in their basic order: the patriarchs, the exodus, and the occupation of the land. These liturgical formulas serve various functions. In Deut. 26:5–9 the themes occur in a confession of faith to be recited by the Israelite farmer prior to his offering a prayer (26:10) when he brings to God the first fruits to ripen in his fields. Deuteronomy 6:20–25 places the confession in the instruction which a father gives to his son. In Josh. 24:2–13 the themes are developed more fully in a formal address in which Yahweh himself, through a prophetic spokesman, reminds Israel of the manner in which the tribal league came to be established. These three forms show that the basic data of the promise to the patriarchs, the deliverance from Egypt, and the gift of the land were recited on various occasions —when an individual gave thanks for the harvest, in family instruction, and on occasions when all Israel was involved. In this way we not only find confirmation of a preliterary transmission of materials, but beyond that, students of the history of transmission think that these liturgically ordered celebrations in the early period of Israel's history may even be the source of the Pentateuch in its basic outline.

Many details remain obscure about the groups that transmitted the material and the places where it was transmitted, but even so we can be sure of the basic fact of transmission, and it is confirmed by a startling observation. In the formulas just discussed there is no mention of the Sinai tradition, which in our present Pentateuch occupies such a large place between the exodus and the occupation of the land, in the midst of the accounts of the wilderness period. This seems clearly to indicate that at an early period the revelation at Sinai and the giving of the law were transmitted separately from the other material. They must have been preserved in connection with other occasions and perhaps even by different groups. Various theories are currently being advanced concerning this matter. Here it is enough to observe that the necessity of investigating the groups and places involved in preliterary transmission of the material can no longer be disputed.

The relation of tradition to history is complicated. Consider the Passover tradition of Exod. 12:21 ff. as an example. This tradition takes up a ritual practiced by seminomads, who each spring move out of the steppes into the cultivated land where they and their herds can find food during the dry months of the year. In order to prevent the envious demons of the wilderness from hindering them, each family sacrifices an animal and sprinkles its blood on the tent posts. In Israel this custom was taken over to serve as a reminder of the departure from Egypt. The ritual specified the spring season, the sacrificial liturgy, and the family as the locus of the observance. But the function of apotropaic magic, which was of great importance to the nomads moving from the steppes, was dropped. The task instead was one of representing a historically unique event of fundamental significance, Yahweh's saving action during the exodus from Egypt. The historical nucleus is then the deliverance at the Sea of Reeds, but the foundation of the tradition rests on a ritual connected with the spring migrations of seminomads. The tradition is preserved in the Israelite Passover festival.

It is in this way that research in the history of tradition pushes back into the preliterary transmission of the material, with the result that various textual emphases are seen more clearly against the background of the transmission of the materials that make up the text. We have illustrated this with examples of separate accounts, but the same holds generally true of the oldest literary sources as a whole.

This study of tradition history enables us to compare the Yahwist and the Elohist. Both presuppose the traditions of the patriarchs, the exodus, Sinai, the wilderness wandering, and the occupation of the land. The details of the parallel accounts are instructive, from Abraham's denial that Sarah is his wife (see above, p. 22), on to the final major complex of stories belonging to the tradition about the occupation of the land, namely, the Balaam stories in Numbers 22–24, which in chapter 23 are Elohistic and in chapter 24 are Yahwistic.

The Yahwist

On close inspection, the Yahwist is seen to have a distinctive way of arranging his total composition. In contrast to the Elohist, he prefaces his stories of the patriarchs with a group of stories about human history generally and the history of the nations. At the beginning, in Gen. 2:4b–3:24, he speaks of creation and the fall of the first man and woman. Man, in Hebrew *adam,* is related to the ground, *adamah,* in three ways. He is created out of it (2:7); because of his lack of trust in the gifts that God has given him (2:15; 3:2 ff.) he can draw nourishment from it only by the greatest efforts (3:17–18); and finally, as dust he must go back to it at last (3:19). In 4:1–16 the Yahwist explains why the Kenites must live an unsettled, fugitive life —because of the murder committed by their ancestor. In the account of the great flood, the goodness of God that preserves all things triumphs in the end, in spite of man's unchanging evil (cf. Gen. 6:6 ff.; 8:21 f.). The story of Noah and his vineyard shows the dangers of the advance in civilization represented by viniculture (Gen. 9:20 ff.), and at the same time the reprehensible sexual looseness of the ancestor of the Canaanites (9:22–

25). The building of the city and the tower of Babylon discloses mankind's arrogance and self-will, which bring with them the curse whereby men are no longer able to communicate with each other (11:1–9). The Yahwist opens his work with these major accounts and some lesser ones. Each link in this remarkable chain has its own prehistory, and they all point to an origin outside of Israel. Thus the Yahwist expresses something in his total composition that was not found in any old Israelite credo, family instruction, or testimony used in praise of Yahweh at the great festival gatherings.

In other respects too the Yahwist seems quite modern. He has questions about the remarkable relationship of the sexes to each other (Gen. 2:18 ff.; 3:6 ff.), the coexistence of city dwellers and bedouin (4:17 ff.), the origin of musicians and metalworkers (4:21–22), the disruptive consequences of the development of viniculture (9:20 ff.), the multiplicity of nations with their separate territories (10:8 ff.), and the technical possibilities of giant construction projects (11:3). His many-sided interest in the history of culture is, however, subordinate to his purpose of expressing a specific point of view: mankind lives in mistrust and pride, and, as a result, in pain, discord, and anxiety. For this reason Yahweh has set bounds for mankind. Nonetheless he lets man live in hope for the future.

For the Yahwist this future began with Yahweh's promise to Abraham, "By you all the families of the earth shall bless themselves" (Gen. 12:2*b*). This saying casts new light on the old Israelite traditional material by relating it specifically to the nations that were incorporated into the empire of David and Solomon. It is this period that the Yahwist is apparently addressing. He does not stop, however, with showing the nations under a curse, like the descendants of Cain in Gen. 9:25, the bedouin Kenites in 4:11 ff., or those involved in the confusion of languages in 11:7 ff. He is concerned to remind a victorious Israel that, since the time of the patriarchs, it has enriched the life of the foreign nations that it has now subjugated. The Ammonites and Moabites had benefited by Abraham's intercession (Gen. 18:17 ff., 25; cf. 19:37 f.). Isaac had made a treaty of peace with the Philistines (26:1 ff., 27 ff.). Jacob had given economic help to the Arameans (30:27 ff.). And Joseph, through his political skill, had provided food for a whole world of hungry people (39:5; 47:13–26). Even the exodus tradition sheds new light on the Yahwist's general theme—blessing for everyone comes from Israel. In the story of the plagues he shows how oppression of the Hebrews brought a curse on the Egyptians. But at the end, after the firstborn have been killed, Pharaoh's last words are, "Rise up, go forth from among my people . . . and go, serve the Lord. . . . and bless me also!" (Exod. 12:31–32). This request, made in consequence of Israel's having been saved, would in the empire of David and Solomon be fulfilled for the world around Israel. Even the major powers are included in it. Thus the Yahwist places the primal history at the beginning and stresses that Israel will be a blessing to all the nations. He does this in connection with his use of the traditional material in order to set new goals before his contemporaries.

In spite of his obviously modern spirit, his method of narration is deeply indebted to the material handed down to him. He took over almost unchanged the myth about giants originating through marriage between the sons of the gods and the daughters of men, leaving all initiative in the matter with the sons of the gods (Gen. 6:1–4). Only by the material inserted in v. 3 and by the larger context does he show the purpose of preserving this story—he wants to give one additional example of human *hubris*. The tensions produced by the old material bothered him less than reworking them would have.

His view of God also impresses us as archaic. Yahweh walks "in the cool of the day" and searches for man behind the bushes (Gen. 3:8 f.). He lets Abraham serve him a large feast (18:6 ff.). Such mythical, anthropomorphic ways of speaking did not bother the Yahwist. That Yahweh comes to men, associates with them, works for them as potter (2:7), gardener (2:8), or tailor (3:21), and calls to men in a way that cannot be ignored—this is more important to the Yahwist than any efforts to think metaphysically.

The Elohist

The Elohist is quite different. His method of narration, for example, is different from that of the Yahwist. The way he reworked the traditional material about the threat to the ancestral mother is a case in point. In Gen. 12:10–20 the Yahwist had only two bits of dialogue. At the beginning Abraham told Sarah to say that she was his sister, and at the end Pharaoh called Abraham to account. In between, what happened to Sarah and how Yahweh intervened are described in detail. The Elohist, on the other hand, used dialogue to express everything that is essential to the story. God explains to Abimelech in a dream the guilt that he is in danger of bringing on himself (Gen. 20:3). Abimelech excuses himself by recounting what had happened (20:4 f.). Then God speaks again and gives advice on how to resolve the problem (20:6 f.). When Abimelech gives Abraham's wife back he speaks to Abraham twice, Abraham answers, and then Abimelech has a final word to Abraham and Sarah (20:9–16). It is worth noting that when Abraham speaks he recalls the time he left his homeland: "When God caused me to wander from my father's house, I said to her, 'This is the kindness you must do me: at every place to which we come, say of me, He is my brother' " (20:13). An account corresponding to this reminiscence of Abraham's departure seems to have been sacrificed by the editors who combined this material with that of the Yahwist. This linking of formerly separate narratives is typical of the Elohist. Typical also are summary statements, as in Joseph's final words to his brothers, "As for you, you meant evil against me; but God meant it for good" (Gen. 50:20). So we see that the Elohist typically interweaves his own thought with the material at hand by means of extensive dialogue, and that he seeks to articulate the significance of large contexts.

In this way a more reflective theology arose in which God appears more distant. God speaks to Abimelech in a dream (Gen. 20:3, 6); only a ladder binds heaven and earth together (Gen. 28:11 f.). God uses an angel to rescue Israel from the Egyptians (Exod. 14:19). Joseph discovers that even in the intrigues of his brothers God was secretly at work. Thus does the Elohist deal intensively with the problem of the hiddenness of God. It is not accidental that we are indebted to the Elohist for the only explanation of the name Yahweh, in Exod. 3:14, "I reveal myself as the one who reveals himself" (see above, p. 17). Where and how God is at work in Israel's history can be discovered only through the agency of human witnesses. In the story of Sinai the Elohist shows that such use of intermediaries is the compassionate answer to the people's anxious request to Moses, "You speak to us, and we will hear; but let not God speak to us, lest we die" (Exod. 20:19). Only because an intermediary is allowed can Israel live within, and in spite of, its knowledge of God. Without an intermediary, there would be only the alternatives of death or living without a knowledge of God.

What is the purpose of this mediated knowledge of God? In Israel's traditions the Elohist finds the answer in the message peculiar to him: the fear of God is so to govern those who hear the message that they are enabled to give proper obedience—and appropriate disobedience. Moses explains God's appearing on Mount Sinai by saying, "God has come to prove you, and that the fear of him may be before your eyes, that you may not sin" (Exod. 20:20). Abraham himself sounded this note in the first of the major Elohistic accounts when he told Abimelech, "I thought there is no fear of God at all in this place" (Gen. 20:11). Fear of God prompted the midwives in Egypt to passive resistance against the command of the king to kill all boys born to Hebrew women (Exod. 1:17, 21). One of the major points to which the Elohist bears testimony is that Israel became a people only through a political disobedience engendered by their fear of God. Israel's entire history is seen as a series of tests of obedience, the most moving example being the famous Elohistic story of the temptation of Abraham. By his readiness to sacrifice even the son of promise—and with him the promised future of his people—Abraham displayed his fear of God (Gen. 22:1-12).

They must have been trying times indeed that caused the Elohist to attend so intently to the witness of the patriarchs as a way of discerning the proper road for God's people to travel. He left untouched the stories of mankind and of the nations, stories which the Yahwist had used during the days of the empire. In spite of its interpretations being couched in terms of the ancient confessions, the advanced stage of reflection indicates that this Elohistic material is not as old as that of the Yahwist. The inhabitants of the northern kingdom in the century between Elijah and Hosea (ninth to eighth century B.C.) underwent innumerable tests of their obedience. Kings used alien systems to suppress ancient Israelite liberties (1 Kings 21), social crises threatened the law (Amos 5). The Elohist's call to fear God was addressed directly to these highly threatened generations.

I AM YOUR GOD, AND YOU ARE MY PEOPLE:
THE PRIESTLY DOCUMENT AND DEUTERONOMY

The Priestly Document

In the Pentateuch there is a third narrative strand distinguishable from those of the Yahwist and the Elohist. We have already seen that this third strand surrounds the older literary works like a framework (Gen. 1; Deut. 34:7–10; see above, pp. 7 f.). Because of its interest in cultic matters, scholars call it the "Priestly Document." The editorial method in Israel was to embed indispensable older materials in newer compositions. For this reason we can assume that we have here in their final narrative form the major points of the history of ancient Israel's founding and faith. If one or two centuries elapsed between the earliest work of the Yahwist in the tenth century and that of the Elohist, then certainly another two centuries passed before the priestly narrative took its present form. No adequate evidence can be produced for dating it prior to the exile, that is to say, the middle of the sixth century.

The first thing to note about the Priestly Document is that it again places the beginnings of Israel in the framework of world history. In his concentration on Israel the Elohist had shown no interest in general history. On this score, however, our latest witness resembles more the Yahwist, with whose tales of the nations he interweaves his own stories in the primal history in Genesis 1–11. In his time Israel again had wide horizons. To be sure, it was no longer a center of imperial power as in the days of David and Solomon. Conquered by the neo-Babylonian empire and bereft of its political institutions, land, and Temple, it was leading a marginal existence in a foreign empire. The colorful world of the nations with which the Yahwist had been concerned, e.g., in his treatment of the Kenites, Canaanites, and

Babylonians, disappears behind formal genealogies (Gen. 10:1–7, 20, 22 f., 31 f.; cf. Gen. 5). Only those things that have to do with all mankind are recounted—creation, the flood, and the covenant with Noah. The exiles were hard beset and needed to know that creation was something that God had made for the good of mankind (Gen. 1:31). Definite boundaries have been set for the waters (in Mesopotamia water threatened to bring chaos [1:6–10], whereas on the Canaanite view held by the Yahwist water is not a threat to life but that which makes life possible [2:6]). The heavenly bodies are not to be regarded as arbitrary astral gods but as helps which God has given to man (1:14–18). Man alone is placed in the whole cosmos as the representative (image) of God (1:26–28). The story of the flood (6:9–22; 8:14–19, with many Yahwist insertions) teaches that all men have forfeited their lives by their violence (6:13) but that God, through one righteous man, Noah (6:10), has granted them a new start in life (8:15 ff.). From then on they live by God's tolerance. God's renunciation of total destruction is theologically explained—with an anticipatory parallel to God's promise to Abraham (Gen. 17) and to Israel (Exod. 6)—as a "covenant" with Noah, who is given as a sign of the covenant something that is known around the world: God places the rainbow in the clouds the way an archer hangs his weapon on a nail (Gen. 9:8–17). Israel, scattered among the nations of the world, is to realize that she lives by the goodness of the Creator and by his renunciation of force.

In addition, Israel itself enters into a relationship where it knows God. As foreigners among the nations, the people of Israel are reminded of Abraham (Gen. 17:8). They can remember the movable tabernacle and the transportable ark of the covenant as places where they had met with God (Exod. 25:10 ff.; 29:42 ff.; 40:1 ff.). Above all, they are to recall those signs of the covenant which are essentially different from the bow in the clouds.

Abraham was given circumcision (Gen. 17:10 ff.) as a sign that every individual Israelite belonged to the God of promise (17:4 ff.), and Israel was given the sabbath as a sign of the completion of God's work of providing for his people, a completion that man can celebrate only by total rest from work (Exod. 16:23–30; cf. Gen. 2:1–3; Exod. 31:12–17). Both these signs of the covenant are, in contrast to the sign given to Noah, to be observed by those who know God. Both could be practiced in the diaspora.

The Priestly Document also developed a theology according to which every event was the result of a word of God. "And God said, 'Let there be light'; and there was light" (Gen. 1:3). And so, for example, when the covenant is made with Noah (Gen. 9) and with Abraham (17:1–16) only the word of God is reported. And the carrying out of instructions is recounted in the same words (e.g., Num. 27:15–21, 22 f.; Exod. 25–29, 35–39). This consistent theology of the word of God was probably inspired by the prophetic messages, which attracted increased attention in the exile (Isa. 40:8; 55:10 f.). It made people more alert to the active force of Yahweh's words of promise and command in the older Pentateuch traditions.

As its vital message for its day, the Priestly Document stressed the first of the two statements in the covenant formula: I am your God, you are my people. Israel had not measured up to the requirements of living as Yahweh's people, and so they had lost their land, nation, and Temple. After being punished (cf. Isa. 40:2) they are now to recall that God had committed himself to them, and that the covenant which he had instituted remained in force even though Israel had broken it (cf. Jer. 31:31–34; Ezek. 36:22–32). Thus, so far as the content of the covenant is concerned, the Priestly Document stressed Yahweh's promise, "I will establish my covenant . . . to be God to you and to your descendants after you" (Gen. 17:7, 8; Exod. 29:45–

46). It is characteristic that the second half of the covenant formula, when it occurs at all, is reformulated through changing the subject, and then is subordinated to the first half: "And I will take you for my people, and I will be your God; and you shall know that I am the Lord your God, who has brought you out from under the burdens of the Egyptians" (Exod. 6:7). In this way the people of Israel, living under foreign domination, were to gain a new understanding of the exodus tradition. The celebration of the Passover, instead of being centrally located as in Deuteronomy 16 (see below, p. 42), was again to take place in the family. So observed, it could awaken the hopes of the small scattered groups in the diaspora (cf. Exod. 12:11–14 with Isa. 52:10–12).

EXCURSUS: *Literary Criticism*

The new formulation of the exodus tradition in the Priestly Document affords an appropriate context in which to explain the literary-critical method. For this purpose we might look at the parallel accounts of the call of Moses.

The necessity of considering literary-critical questions arises from the fact that in Exod. 2:23–6:8 the material is reported three times and the texts are closely interwoven. A comparison of the addresses to Moses in 3:7–8; 3:9–10; and 6:2–8 shows that in each instance God says concerning himself that he has become aware of the plight of his people Israel in Egypt (3:7, 9; 6:5) and that he intends to lead them out of Egypt (3:8, 10; 6:6). The question at once arises why we should assume here that literary strands have been interwoven rather than that preliterary traditions have been brought together, as was the case in the threefold report of the threat to the ancestral mother (see above, p. 22). There the material had been taken up into different circles of tradition, the traditions about Abraham and those about Isaac. As a result, the literary composition took place in widely separated realms. In one of the literary strands the same material could occur twice, some distance apart (Gen. 12 and 26, the Yahwist). In the same circle of tradition it could take on two different literary forms, with the clearly observable peculiarities of speech and viewpoint of the Yahwist (Gen. 12) and the Elohist (Gen. 20). In Exodus 3–6, however, we remain within a unified complex of material, the call of Moses, where the identity of content has already been demonstrated. The threefold parallel makes it probable as a working hypothesis that the same material was formulated by each of the three sources (Yahwist, Elohist, and Priestly Document) and later combined editorially. We must carefully seek to determine whether the present composition can be better explained in terms of literary sources or as the first deposit of oral tradition.

After establishing that slightly different parallels have been closely woven together, we must next look for differences in language which may indicate the possible existence of earlier written sources. We observe that in the three texts in question the plight of the Israelites is described in terms of three different words: "affliction" (3:7), "oppression" (3:9), and "bondage" (6:6). At the same time the sentences in which these words appear show only minor differences. Still, the manner in which the Israelites' lament over their plight and Yahweh's attention to them are depicted substantiate the assumption of literary parallels. Verse 7 is the most detailed and concrete: "I have seen the affliction of my people who are in Egypt, and have heard their cry because of their taskmasters; I know their sufferings." And since vv. 8 and 10 each speak of the plan for saving Israel, the assumption seems unavoidable that 3:7–8 and 3:9–10 belong to different sources. The details in 6:5 are given concisely, even though the context, vv. 2–8, is consistently well developed. "I have heard the groaning of the people of Israel whom the Egyptians hold in bondage, and I have remembered my covenant." How could these instances of divergent vocabulary and parallel content be explained if they did not go back to written sources?

Differences in point of view strengthen the case and make it possible to identify the sources. The last of the three texts says that Yahweh "remembered" the covenant (6:5*b*), thereby indicating that it is a part of the Priestly Document. The reference is to the establishment of the covenant with Abraham and the promise to give his descendants "the land in which they dwelt as sojourners" (cf. Exod. 6:4 with Gen. 17:7–8). The beginning of the passage, Exod. 6:2, is typical of the Priestly Document: "God said to Moses, 'I am the Lord. I appeared to Abraham, to Isaac, and to Jacob, as God Almighty [El Shaddai], but by my name the Lord [Yahweh] I did not make myself known to them." In the framework we find the term "God," as we do generally in the Priestly Document (Gen. 1, 9, 17; Exod. 2:23–25). In God's speech to Moses there is a transition from the name El Shaddai (which God used in speaking to Abraham in Gen. 17:1) to "Yahweh." The various names used for God enable us to begin to analyze the two parallel strands. In Exod. 3:7 the first words are "Then the Lord [Yahweh] said." Here as elsewhere that is a clear indication that the passage comes from the Yahwist. The parallel in 3:9–10 does not start with an introductory formula. It does continue, however, without interruption, to say in vv. 11 ff., "But Moses said to God [Elohim]" —a sure sign of the Elohist. And when this phrase is followed directly by the revelation of the name of Yahweh what we have is a clear example of how models are used by the Priestly Document (see above, p. 30).

The differing concepts of God, however, are an even clearer indication of the separate sources than is the use of different names for God. Note here how rescue is promised. In 3:8 we read, "I have come down to deliver them out of the hand of the Egyptians." In v. 10, however, God tells Moses, "Come, I will send you to Pharaoh that you may bring forth my people, the sons of Israel, out of Egypt." It is hard to imagine a more typical juxtaposition of Yahwist and Elohist. When the tower of Babel was being built, "The Lord came down" (Gen. 11:5, Yahwist); in Gen. 18:21 he says that he himself will "go down" to Sodom (Yahwist); and in Exod. 19:20, "The Lord came down upon Mount Sinai"—again the Yahwist. The same Hebrew word in all three cases indicates the anthropomorphic theology of the Yahwist, in which Yahweh himself comes down to earth and is concerned about human beings (see above, p. 29). In contrast, in Exod. 3:9–10, as is typical of the Elohist, God keeps his distance and makes use of a messenger, in this instance Moses (see above, p. 30). It is not Yahweh but Moses who leads Israel out of Egypt. The Priestly Document, on the other hand, sees the exodus as the fulfillment of the covenant made with Abraham (6:4). The events of the exodus are interpreted primarily as the beginning of the gift of the land—the land where the patriarchs were strangers will be Israel's own possession (6:8). This was the message to the community in exile. The Yahwist, on the other hand, spoke of the "good and broad land" (3:8) because the extent and fertility of the land were of greater concern to the people in Solomon's day than was the tradition according to which the patriarchs had lived in the land as sojourners.

Literary criticism fulfills its purpose only when an individual passage can be assigned to a larger context in terms of the literary purpose of that context. A comparison between what is stressed in the proclamation of the individual passage and in that of the larger context serves as an objective control of this process. The account in 6:2–8 brings the message of vv. 5–6—

that God notes the people's plight and promises deliverance—into unmistakable agreement with the specific priestly message when it adds in v. 7, "I will take you for my people, and I will be your God; and you shall know that I am the Lord your God" (see above, p. 34). The Elohist in 3:10 calls for Moses to be obedient. In 3:6*b* it had been said of Moses that "he hid his face, for he was afraid to look at God." This agrees with the Elohistic emphasis on fear of God (see above, pp. 30 f.). The Yahwist's message of blessing is found in this fragment only in the mention of the goal of the "good and broad land" (3:8). The wider context makes it clear that resistance to Yahweh's purpose of saving his people brings a curse on Egypt (see the account of the plagues in 7:14 ff.), and that submission would bring blessing even for Pharaoh (12:32; see above, p. 28).

Besides seeking to separate the various sources, literary criticism must also investigate the way in which the sources were put together, that is to say, the editorial process. Our example here shows that the Yahwist and the Elohist had been brought together before the time of the Priestly Document (3:1–6:1); in their conjunction they were taken up into the younger document (cf. 2:23–25 with 6:2 ff.). The older strands were so closely united that the reader understood the Elohist's commission to Moses (3:10) as the result of the will of Yahweh expressed by the Yahwist in 3:8. Since, however, the two accounts with their distinctive formulations of the reasons for Moses' call—which correspond to the Yahwistic and Elohistic theologies—were both included, we can still recognize that two sources lie behind this composition. The "and now" in 3:9 is a clever editorial connective. The editors who combined the Yahwist-Elohist document with the Priestly Document allowed the older sources to continue down to the failure of the first encounter with Pharaoh (chaps. 3–5). As a result, the priestly parallel in 6:2 ff. appears to be a new call to Moses. But the wording and point of view connect it with the strand in 2:23–25.

In many cases it is not clear whether literary or oral traditions were combined. Anyone who investigates the history of transmission must assume that either may have taken place.

Deuteronomy

The Priestly Document embraces not only the Yahwist-Elohist work and various other additions but also, by its account of the death of Moses (Deut. 34:7–9), the Deuteronomic book of the law as well (Deut. 4:44–28:44), a book which derives its name as "second law" from the reference in Deut. 17:18 to a "copy of the law." The book of Deuteronomy bracketed this older law book within a framework of speeches by later devotees of the same school (1:1–4:43; 28:45–30:10), thereby making it the primary document in the "Deuteronomic history" (see below, p. 54).

The outline of the Deuteronomic law is clear. In the middle (chaps. 12–26) we have a collection of interpretations of the law. They are introduced by sermons in chapters 6–11, to which the Decalogue (chap. 5) serves as a preface. Lists of blessings and curses are found at the end (chaps. 27–28). The book is unquestionably the result of oral recitation, and its outline may even reflect a liturgical formula.

Its origin is to be sought in the circles of Levitical preachers who spiritually were very close to the prophet Hosea. At least in part, Deuteronomy as a literary document served as the basis of the religious reforms of King Josiah in 622 B.C. (2 Kings 22–23). It must therefore have had its origin in the seventh century. Various strands can be recognized by the variation between singular and plural in sections where the hearer is addressed. There is still considerable dispute about details of the literary problems.

The theological principles of this exposition of the law are unmistakable. One main strand stresses the fact that Yahweh's gifts precede Israel's acts of obedience. As a consequence, the offering of sacrifices is not an obligatory and burdensome task but something that they were to do "as much as you desire, according to the blessing of the Lord your God which he has given you" (Deut. 12:15). When a slave was freed in the seventh year, he was to be sent away richly loaded with gifts of cattle, grain, and wine, "as the Lord your God has blessed you" (15:14). The people were to express through their obedience the great joy which they felt over the blessings which the Lord had showered on them. The basis of this blessing is the covenant which Yahweh established at Horeb (5:2 f.; 9:8 f.), but which applies also to the generation that was present there that day (5:3). The whole Deuteronomic book purports to be a new proclamation of the covenant at Sinai, one continuous and complete address by Moses in Moab (4:44 ff.). The other ancient traditions were only aids in characterizing this covenant. It had been promised to the patriarchs, and by the deliverance out of the house of bondage in Egypt and by the gift of the promised land (7:1 ff., 7 ff.) was shown to be a freely given covenant of love. As a guarantee of his abiding presence, God would "put his name" (12:5) or "let his name dwell" at a chosen place (12:11; 14:23–24; 16:2, 6, 11; 26:2). So it is that following the anthropomorphic theology of the Yahwist, and building somewhat upon the Elohist's theology of a mediator, and prior to the priestly theology of the word of God, there makes its first appearance in Israel here in Deuteronomy a theology of the covenant and a theology of the "name of Yahweh."

The chief concern of the message of Deuteronomy is to appeal to Israel to be "a people holy to the Lord your God" (7:6; 14:2; 16:18 f.). In this way the second half of the covenant formula, "You are Yahweh's people," becomes the central theme of the proclamation, in contrast to the later Priestly Document (see above, p. 35). The Deuteronomic writers took up the message of judgment which the prophets had proclaimed; they worked zealously to make the people heed it and remain in a state of well-being. Every true prophet was regarded as a Moses come back to life (18:15 ff.). They issued a concrete call to the people to forsake the innumerable cultic sites in the land and gather in the one place which Yahweh had chosen as the place where his name would dwell (12:2 ff.; 16:1 ff.). They showed compassion for the social problems of the poor and of slaves (15:7 ff., 12 ff.)—witness the basis given for the command to keep the sabbath (5:14; cf. Exod. 20:11). Even the king is placed on a level with the brethren who must listen to Yahweh (Deut. 17:14 ff.); he is not to distinguish himself from them by military power, a huge harem, or the amassing of a fortune, but by devoted study of the Torah, God's law. The curses in 28:15 ff. reflect the greatest danger facing Israel, the danger of losing the blessings of the covenant by ignoring the voice of Yahweh.

Other Pentateuchal Laws

In addition to Deuteronomy, the Pentateuch contains numerous smaller legal codes and collections of laws.

The oldest of these is the "Book of the Covenant" in Exod. 20:22–23:19. In part its stipulations are reworked in Deuteronomy. Following ancient oriental traditions the Book of the Covenant presents legal materials in specific order. These materials presuppose the life of the tribes after the conquest but before the founding of the national government.

A later collection of laws, probably not far in point of time from Deuteronomy itself, is found in Leviticus 17–26. It is called the "Holiness Code" because of its basic theme, repeated in various formulations, "You shall be holy; for I the Lord your God am holy" (19:2). The Holiness Code includes a variety of ancient material, as is shown by the specification in Leviticus 18 of the limits of sexual relationships in the nomadic extended family. In Leviticus there are also rules similar in content to the Ten Commandments, but in smaller lists of two to four units.

The Forms of Law

In the various collections of laws we encounter two basic forms: casuistic regulations and normative requirements.

The casuistic regulations present a case in the first clause and then give the punishment prescribed for it. This form is found in many ancient oriental law codes, for example, the code of Hammurabi. In this type of law, Israel probably borrowed extensively from the regular legal practice of the Canaanite cities.

Normative requirements are found in both brief and long lists. For condemned behavior they either prescribe the death penalty, as the list shows that is included in the Book of the Covenant (Exod. 21:12, 15–17; 22:18 f.), or they pronounce a curse, as in the list of twelve curses in Deut. 27:15–26. They command or prohibit in apodictic manner, without qualification, as in the Decalogue in Exodus 20 and Deuteronomy 5, or the smaller ancient series preserved in Leviticus 19. This fundamental, normative law safeguards the area of freedom by establishing its limits. It takes the form of a series of commands, and its content is typical of Israel, especially its prohibition of the worship of foreign gods and images. This is the basic command that delimits and liberates the secular life which is the subject of the other regulations.

Ritual Requirements

In addition, the Pentateuch contains a large number of ritual requirements, for example, the rules governing sacrifices in Leviticus 1–7 and those governing ritual purity in Leviticus 11–15. In some places contemporary scholarship can demonstrate that these rules are the result of stubborn resistance to the inroads of foreign cults which sought to lure the Israelites out of the realm of freedom that Yahweh had given to them. Through the texts discovered at Ras Shamra (see below, pp. 137 f.) we know now that in the ancient city of Ugarit the wild boar was closely associated with the god Aliyan Baal, who was worshiped there. Leviticus 11:7 declares that swine are unclean. Similarly 11:4 declares that the camel is unclean, thereby making clear the cultic distinction between Israel and the camel-riding nomads. Through all these cultic instructions, almost all of which seem strange to us, there runs a restrained passion for the purification and liberation of the totality of everyday life.

REPENTANCE AND SEPARATION: THE DEUTERONOMIC HISTORY AND THE WORK OF THE CHRONICLER

The Writing of History

In writing its major works of history Israel followed in general a course unique in the ancient Near East and the entire ancient world. The oldest documents show us that Israel first met her God Yahweh in the wide area of secular history. Yahweh gave Israel its own history among the nations. In this history God spoke and acted with Israel, and so set in motion his history on behalf of all mankind. This is the reason why the song of Miriam praised him and the basic statements in the old confessional formulas honored him; and this is the way in which the Yahwist and the Priestly Document portrayed him. Still the major literary forms of the Pentateuch were more in the nature of confessions of faith than history in the strict sense. To be sure, the transition is gradual, for it was a clear consciousness of history that guided the Yahwist in his presentation of the irreversible changes in the course of human life. But a few characteristic points may be noted. The outlines of the Pentateuchal documents were determined by the great themes of the "credo" and not by a primarily historical interest. In the individual stories more attention was given to the words and marvelous deeds of Yahweh than to any specific profile of human history; a history which had not yet been identified could hardly be conceptualized. As a result, the Pentateuchal source material took the form of rather loosely united collections of typological examples or etiological stories. These examples and stories were thought of as having kerygmatic significance for larger contexts, and the compilers were not interested in investigating immanent causes and consequences.

What was still lacking is found in the Deuteronomic history, indeed already in its sources. An identifiable course of history determines the presentation of material, interest in miracles is far outweighed by the penetrating observation of human powers and their nature, and the individual scene is caught up in the context of the events occurring in the stream of history.

Since the Deuteronomic history made careful use of the older literary sources we are able to observe the main stages in ancient Israelite writing of history. There was a change in the way the testimony to Yahweh was presented. We can identify and illustrate five phases.

The first and most direct testimony is the song. Songs let later generations participate in a historical event at the hour of its birth. When David returned victorious from fighting the Philistines the women danced and sang, "Saul has slain his thousands, and David his ten thousands!" (1 Sam. 18:7). This song even crossed the border—the Philistines used it to describe David: "Is not this David, of whom they sing to one another in dances, 'Saul has slain his thousands, and David his ten thousands'?" (1 Sam. 29:5; cf. 21:12). Consisting of only five Hebrew words, this song transports every reader back into the excitement Israel felt at David's victories over the Philistines. It reveals the historical cause of the tensions between Saul and David and the reason why the young David was a favorite of the people. In similar manner the song of Deborah in Judges 5 brings its hearers into the tumult of the war between the Israelite tribes under Barak and the Canaanite troops under Sisera. Against the background of the clearly depicted quarrels and foibles of the tribal league, Yahweh is praised as the one who really did the fighting and conquering. (For a discussion of the song of Miriam, see above, p. 8.)

Second is the anecdote. Preserving individual facts that could not have been invented, anecdotes for a brief moment illuminate a whole scene. Judges 12:1 ff. reports a struggle between the tribes in Gilead east of the Jordan River under Jephthah, and the tribe of Ephraim west of the Jordan. Gilead defeated Ephraim and occupied the fords of the Jordan. Soldiers were posted at the fords to capture Ephraimite fugitives. An infallible identification was provided by a difference in dialect. The soldiers ordered anyone wanting to cross the border to say "Shibboleth!"—a word meaning "sheaves." If he pronounced it "sibboleth" he was exposed as an Ephraimite and killed on the spot (12:6). Such was the enmity among those who were supposed to stick together as God's people Israel, and the narrator makes this point with an anecdote. According to its etymology, "anecdote" means "not given out." An anecdote is not something published but something picked up, an individual unit that has been transmitted orally. Anecdotes are particularly known for preserving characteristic statements. In the accounts of the beginning of Saul's kingdom we find the statement: "Some worthless fellows said, 'How can this man save us?' And they despised him, and brought him no present" (1 Sam. 10:27). This clearly preserves something of historical relevance, the fact that the monarchy was not established in Israel without opposition. The evaluation of the speakers as "worthless fellows" indicates the internal tensions of the times. The statement, however, served the purpose of the later Deuteronomic criticism of the monarchy (cf. 1 Sam. 8:7) by indicating that Yahweh's kingship had been rejected.

At the third stage we encounter the episode. Episodes depict an isolated context of events. Judges 9, for example, reports the origins of Abimelech's kingdom, its establishment in Shechem, and its early downfall. In similar manner the collapse of Solomon's empire under his son Rehoboam is presented in 1 Kings 12:1–19 in a historically credible report of the gathering in Shechem. The collapse is then explained as the work of Yahweh by recalling a message of the prophet Ahijah of Shilo, which makes explicit the viewpoint of the narrator.

In the time of Solomon we have, as a fourth stage, the first presentation of a history of the times in a larger context. This history of the times incorporated the isolated remembrances of songs, anecdotes, and episodes into the writing of history. Two accounts were developed in this manner, the story of David's rise to power (1 Sam. 16:14–2 Sam. 5:10) and that of the struggles over the succession to his throne (2 Sam. 6:23–1 Kings 2:46). The human causes and effects are identified. Yahweh's miraculous intervention receded into the background. This made it all the more clear that the confusion of events—both instances depict the disturbances accompanying a transfer of royal power from one generation to another—can be solved only by Yahweh himself. The story of David's rise begins with the words, "Now the Spirit of the Lord departed from Saul," and it concludes with the words, "And David became greater and greater, for the Lord, the God of hosts, was with him." These marginal comments reveal the beginnings of an interest in the larger context. Only indirectly, by the introduction of the prophet Nathan (2 Sam. 7; 1 Kings 1:11 ff.), is it shown that in the struggle for the succession to the throne of David the changing fortune of the candidates is determined by the word of Yahweh. Belief in the sovereignty of the word of Yahweh allows the writer of history to portray even the great David without touching him up or concealing his human weaknesses and errors, that is, to portray him in a historically reliable way (2 Sam. 11–12).

At the fifth stage we encounter the annals of the court. Such annals are a prerequisite for the writing of a history that covers many generations. They begin with the "book of the acts of Solomon" (1 Kings 11:41) and are continued on the one hand in the "Book of the Chronicles of the kings of Israel" (1 Kings 14:19), and on the other hand with the "Book of the Chronicles of the Kings of Judah" (1 Kings 14:29). In these passages we are given, in addition to the name of the king and that of his mother, his age on ascending the throne, the duration of his reign, events of national and international importance, and often the location of his grave. These court diaries had their forerunners in the lists of the judges (Judg. 10:1–5; 12:7–15).

EXCURSUS: *The Chronological Framework of the History of Israel*

The royal annals are an important aid to chronology. In this sketch we will present those dates that are essential for an understanding of the history of Israel in the context of the ancient world of the Near East. Three major periods are distinguished in the paragraphs which follow: the premonarchical period, the monarchy, and the era of the Jewish religious community.

In the thirteenth and twelfth centuries, at the time of the transition from the Late Bronze Age to the Iron Age, Israelite seminomadic tribes settled in the territory west and east of the Jordan River. They had come out of the steppes to the east and the south. Some groups had been vassals of Rameses II (1290–23) in the New Kingdom of Egypt. About 1220 "Israel" is mentioned for the first time on a stele set up by Pharaoh Merneptah after his military campaign in Palestine. The Israelites are referred to as a weak group of peoples. As Egypt's power waned in the twelfth century sea peoples occupied the coast. They were "Philistines" and gave their name to the land as "Palestine." At the same time the Israelite tribes were settling in the mountainous areas of the ancient territory of the Canaanite states. War flared up with the Canaanites and the camel-riding nomads. Around the end of the eleventh century the militia of the tribes of Israel, still bound by only weak political ties, proved ineffective against the organization and weapons of the Philistines. As a result, under Samuel, the last of the "judges," Saul's military kingdom was established.

Israel was first organized as a nation under David (1004–965), who conquered Jerusalem and made it his residence. Under David, Jerusalem became the metropolis of an empire, for the first and only time in the history of the Near East. After David conquered the Philistines and the city-states of Canaan he went on to conquer the Arameans, Ammonites, Moabites, and Edomites, so that his empire stretched from the region of the Euphrates as far as the bounds of the Nile Delta. By taking the ark of the covenant to Jerusalem, he elevated the city to the status of cultic center for the nation, although the Temple was not built until the time of Solomon, being dedicated around 955. After the death of Solomon the empire broke up around

926 into the states of Judah (the southern kingdom under Rehoboam) and Israel (the northern kingdom under Jeroboam I). David's descendants reigned in Jerusalem for over four hundred years. In the north, however, there were only two significant attempts to found dynasties. The first was by Omri, who moved the capital to Samaria, and under whose son Ahab (871–852) the prophet Elijah appeared, and the second was by Jehu (844), whose most significant descendant was Jeroboam II (787–747). Under Tiglath-pileser III (745–727) the neo-Assyrian empire reached out toward Palestine. Arameans and Israelites tried in vain during the Syro-Ephraimite War (733) to force Ahaz of Judah to enter an alliance against Assyria. Meanwhile, Isaiah (736–701) appeared in Jerusalem. As early as 732 the territory of the northern kingdom, except for the hill country of Samaria, had been divided into Assyrian provinces, and in 722 Sargon II conquered this remaining territory and the capital city and annexed it. In 701, during the reign of King Hezekiah, Sennacherib besieged Jerusalem briefly. Then in the second half of the seventh century Assyria's power ended. In 612 its capital, Nineveh, fell. At that time, Judah under King Josiah could for a while reassert its political and religious independence. The reform of worship took place in 622. In less than a decade after the death of Josiah, however, in the reign of Jehoiakim, the emperor Nebuchadnezzar II (604–562) built up the neo-Babylonian empire, conquered Jerusalem in 597, deported King Jehoiachin, and put Zedekiah on the throne in his place. Zedekiah's revolt was punished by the destruction of Jerusalem in 587, after a siege of a year and a half. The prophet Jeremiah was active during the final forty years of the Judean state.

The nation's leaders were taken into exile in Babylon. Among them arose the prophet Ezekiel, and later Second Isaiah, who prophesied the rise of Cyrus II. Cyrus completed the establishment of a Persian empire by the conquest of Babylon in 539, and in 538 he issued an edict liberating the Jews. The first large groups, however, did not return until the reign of his son Cambyses (529–522) at the time of his invasion of Egypt (525). Haggai and Zechariah encouraged the reconstruction of the Temple (520–515) under Darius I (521–485). The efforts of Ezra increased the size of the community of returned exiles and led to their renewal. Either before or after him, Nehemiah, as Persian governor for Judah (445–433), rebuilt the walls of Jerusalem. Alexander the Great conquered the Persian Empire and, in 332, Palestine as well. At this time the Samaritan community consolidated itself on Mount Gerazim near Shechem. In the third century the Ptolemies ruled Palestine; the Torah was translated into Greek. In the second century the Seleucids pushed south as far as Jerusalem, their king, Antiochus IV Epiphanes (175–163), desecrated the Temple, and the Maccabees led the resistance against him. In these troubled times the Book of Daniel appeared, prior to the rededication of the Jerusalem Temple by Judas Maccabeus in December 164. And with this the period of Old Testament Israel came to an end.

The Deuteronomic History

The Deuteronomic history, which includes the books of Deuteronomy, Joshua, Judges, Samuel, and Kings, deals with the history of Israel down to the time of the neo-Babylonian empire, which is apparently as far as its sources went. The message that it proclaims is readily understood in terms of the situation of Israel at that time.

For the dating of the work, it is significant to note that the last event recounted occurred "in the thirty-seventh year of the exile of Jehoiachin" (2 Kings 25:27–30), an exile which began in 597 B.C. The last event is the release of Jehoiachin from prison by Nebuchadnezzar's son Evil-merodach, and his inclusion among those who "dined regularly at the king's table." So the work must be dated later than 561, but not much later, because it makes no mention of the rise of Cyrus to world dominion, a development which involved protracted military campaigns in Asia Minor culminating in the conquest of Babylon in 539. There is no mention of the consequences for Israel, such as the decree of liberation in 538, or of the preceding anticipations, such as we find in Second Isaiah (Isa. 44:28; 45:1–7). Consequently this great history must be dated around 550 B.C.

The problems of authorship are more difficult than those of date. Here two extreme views must be eliminated from consideration. First, it is not a question of a mere editorial reworking of literary materials already at hand. No such materials were available for the latest events, such as the fall of Jerusalem and the exile. More significant, however, is the fact that all the material is artistically assembled and brought into relationship with the basic thoughts of the book of Deuteronomy, which precedes the whole. This was done by speeches and summaries that are clearly related to each other in style and theme. Examples may be found in the speeches of Moses (Deut. 1–4), Joshua (Josh. 1, 23), and Samuel (1 Sam. 12), and in the prayer of Solomon (1 Kings 8). Other examples are the reflections on the results of the conquest of the promised land (Josh. 12), the period of the judges (Judg. 2), the end of the northern kingdom (2 Kings 17), and the fate of Judah (2 Kings 21:10–15), and those in many smaller passages as well. Therefore we are dealing with a carefully composed history which reworked its source material and interpreted the events. This, however, should not lead us to the opposite extreme of assuming that there was a single author of the work. In the major speeches there are unmistakable stylistic tensions (e.g., in Deut. 4 and 1 Kings 8).

In addition, the sources are reworked in varying manner in the major parts of the work. It is probable that the work was produced in several stages by a school which was at work in Judah, and which, because it was a successor to the wisdom literature school that had worked in the court at Jerusalem, may have had access to the material that had been assembled there.

The sources used largely determine the historical sequence of the contents. The Deuteronomic law code, bracketed within a framework of speeches delivered by Moses, is placed at the beginning of the entire work as the essential criterion for the understanding of history. (As a consequence, Deuteronomy today is a focus of discussion for each of two ellipses: within the Pentateuch its claims and demands are subordinated to the saving deeds of Yahweh; in its priority to the books Joshua through Kings, it sets the standards for the history of Israel's preservation and ultimate fall. In the former case it shows the consequences of salvation history, and in the latter case it gives the presuppositions for God's judgments in history.) In the Book of Joshua, etiological stories about various localities such as Gilgal, Jericho, and Ai, primarily localities in the territory of Benjamin, serve as generalized models for the occupation of the land of Israel. For the period of the judges totally different material was available, that which dealt with the great charismatic tribal leaders Gideon (Judg. 6–8) and Samson (Judg. 13–16) being the most prominent. There are also lists of places and boundaries (Josh. 13–21), and a list of the "lesser judges" (Judg. 10:1–5; 12:7–15). The conclusion of the accounts of the judges is found in the stories about Samuel. These include, as an explanation of the wars with the Philistines, the account of the ark of the covenant (1 Sam. 4–6). The conclusion of this account, because of its contents, was placed among the stories of the rise of David and his succession to the throne, in 2 Samuel 6. The arrangement of the material dealing with the beginnings of the monarchy in 1 Samuel 8–12 shows how carefully and skillfully the sources were adapted. Place is given to the expression of quite different positions: an anecdote (10:27), the episode of Saul's war with the Ammonites (11), an old legend of the one who went looking for donkeys and found a kingdom (9–10), and an interpretative reworking of the conflict over the rights of kings in Israel (8; cf. 10:18 f. and chap. 12). From the time of Solomon on, the historian followed the strand of the annals of the royal court. The annals of the northern and southern kingdoms are synchronized, so that the beginning of the reign of a king is identified by the year of the reign of the king in the sister kingdom. The most significant insertions are the short-story-like accounts of prophets, like those about Ahijah of Shilo (1 Kings 11:29–12:20; 14:1–18), Micaiah son of Imlah (1 Kings 22), Elijah (1 Kings 17–19, 21; 2 Kings 1), Elisha (2 Kings 2–13), and Isaiah (2 Kings 18–20).

The main themes of the Deuteronomic understanding of history are revealed in the manner in which the sources were reworked. The blessings and curses of Deuteronomy are connected with the basic thesis that the purity of the worship of Yahweh is to be safeguarded by the centralization of the cult (Deut. 12). And so all the kings of the northern kingdom are accused of the "sin of Jeroboam," which was seen to consist in setting up other cultic sites besides the one that Yahweh had chosen as the place where his name would dwell (1 Kings 12:27 ff.; 13:34; 15:3; and many other passages, down to 2 Kings 17:22). But by forsaking the only God of Israel, Jerusalem too fell short of what was required. The empire collapsed because Solomon acquired a huge harem and let his wives lead him into the worship of many gods (cf. 1 Kings 11:1 ff. with Deut. 17:14 ff. and 7:3 f.). Judah also fell because such kings as Manasseh practiced soothsaying and magic, and set up altars and images of foreign gods in Jerusalem (cf. 2 Kings 21:1–9 with Deut. 17:3; 18:9–14; 12:5, 9 f.).

The other criterion for judging history is the prophetic word. It is found in the stories about the prophets that are inserted in the narrative. The Deuteronomist knew from the separate stories that all important events are the fulfillment of what the prophets had said earlier. Ahab lost the war with the Arameans and died, as prophesied by Micaiah son of Imlah (1 Kings 22:17, 36 f.). In addition, the end of the state of Judah when Jerusalem fell was the fulfillment of Yahweh's word given through the prophets (2 Kings 24:3). In this connection, the prophets were only applying in their time the ancient instructions given by Moses (cf. 1 Kings 2:3; 2 Kings 17:13; 21:1 ff.). In reality all Israel came to ruin because of its failure to honor the words of Moses in Deuteronomy, which were repeated again and again: "The Lord is our God, the Lord alone" (Deut. 6:4).

What was the reason for this great expenditure of energy involved in the writing of a comprehensive history in the midst of the catastrophe of the exile? An oft repeated message bore testimony to Yahweh's righteousness, to the reliability of his word, and to the gleam of hope seen in Jehoiachin's release at the end of the history. This message is: "Return to Yahweh!" At the start of the history we find it in the summary of the address of Moses (Deut. 4:29–31), and later we find it as the summary of the preaching of the prophets (2 Kings 17:13). The total history is traced, because in earlier catastrophes repentance brought a turn of events (Judg. 2:18; 3:9; 1 Sam. 12:20 ff.; 7:3). In the threatened period of exile (Deut. 4:27–31; 1 Kings 8:46–48) it is held up as the only possibility of salvation. In the example of Josiah it is made specific in terms of turning from foreign gods and entering into a new covenant with Yahweh, as specified in Moses' words in Deuteronomy (2

Kings 23:3, 24 f.). The generation that now knew defeat was to find its future way by reflecting on the words that God had spoken earlier and on the reaction of Israel to those words.

The Work of the Chronicler

The work of the chronicler includes the books of 1 and 2 Chronicles, Ezra, and Nehemiah. The Deuteronomic history served as its major source for the period from Saul to Zedekiah, but in Ezra and Nehemiah this new work goes on to recount events of as late as the fifth century. Three distinctive differences between the work of the chronicler and the Deuteronomic history may be mentioned here.

First, David is given far more attention than anyone else. First Chronicles 1–9 offers only genealogies for the time from Adam to Saul. In chapter 10 the death of Saul is reported. All the rest of 1 Chronicles (chaps. 11–29) is devoted to David. Second Chronicles presents Solomon in chapters 1–9, and in 10–26 the time from Rehoboam to the end of the kingdom of Judah and to the decree issued by Cyrus. The books of Ezra and Nehemiah bring the story down to the time of the rebuilding of the walls of Jerusalem under Nehemiah (Neh. 2:1–7:12) and the reorganization of the inner life of the community (Ezra 9; Neh. 8:1–10:13). What is it about David that is of greatest interest? It is the conquest of Jerusalem (1 Chron. 11), the moving of the ark of the covenant (13–16), and the preparations for the building of the Temple and for its equipment and personnel (21–29)—in other words, almost exclusively the cultic institutions of Jerusalem. The stature of David serves to make it all legitimate.

Second, the history of the northern kingdom is practically ignored. It is significant that Jeroboam I is instructed by the Judean king Abijah that "the kingdom of the Lord [is] in the hand of the sons of David" (2 Chron. 13:6–8), and that only in Jerusalem can Yahweh be rightly worshiped.

Third, these differences from the Deuteronomic history make it easy to understand why the development of the postexilic period is included. Ezra 4:6–6:18 contains an account in the Aramaic language of Samaritan resistance to the reconstruction of the Temple in Jerusalem. As a consequence of the enforced movements of peoples under the Assyrians a mixed population had arisen in Samaria (Ezra 4:10). Those who returned to Jerusalem were suspicious of these syncretists, especially since Samaria was the residence of the Persian governor until the time when Nehemiah was made governor of Judah. Ezra brought "the law of the God of heaven" (Ezra 7:12), which constituted the new foundation for the community in Jerusalem. The chronicler was in open opposition to the Samaritan community, which took form around its own cultic life on Mount Gerazim in the fourth century. In contrast to that community, stress was placed on David in order to demonstrate the legitimacy of the worship in Jerusalem, and the northern kingdom is portrayed as a corrupt predecessor of the Samaritans. As a result, this new presentation of history gave support to the pure worship of Yahweh in Jerusalem in late postexilic times.

2. The Future: The Prophetic Books

THE MISSION OF THE PROPHETS: THEIR CALL AND AUTHENTICATION

The prophetic movement is the most astonishing phenomenon of the entire history of Israel. It reached its high point in those figures whose words are collected in the books called the "later prophets"—Isaiah, Jeremiah, Ezekiel, and the Book of the Twelve. The early history of the movement is found in the stories about prophets that are contained in the books of Judges, Samuel, and Kings, which, together with Joshua, are brought together in the Hebrew canon as "earlier prophets." The later history of the movement is found in apocalyptic literature, which begins with the supplements to the writing prophets and is particularly represented in the canon by the Book of Daniel. We may note three outstanding characteristics of these figures called prophets.

The Person of the Prophet

The prophets are regularly introduced by name at the beginning of their writings, and identified by date and place of activity.

The historical person of the prophet assumes fundamental importance for the transmission of his message. The authors of the confessional works and of the works of history remain anonymous; their historical personalities are totally subordinate to their writings. As the originators of a new and unique tradition, however, the prophets establish their own individual worth.

"The words of Amos," "the vision of Isaiah," "the word of the Lord that came to Hosea"—that is the way their writings begin. Why is the name essential? The prophets themselves stress that Yahweh had called them by name. They are given a vision and they hear Yahweh's voice: "Amos, what do you see?" (Amos 7:8; 8:2). Something touches their lips and the voice speaks: "Behold I have put my words in your mouth" (Jer. 1:9). Yahweh's words become identical with human words.

Usually the prophet's place of origin and the place where he is to work are named. "And the Lord took me [Amos of Tekoa] from following the flock, and the Lord said to me, 'Go, prophesy to my people Israel'" (Amos 7:15; cf. 1:1). The dating of the writings was even more important to those who collected them. Amos made his appearance "two years before the earthquake" (Amos 1:1). "In the year that King Uzziah died" (Isa. 6:1) Isaiah saw the Lord. In Jeremiah and Ezekiel dates are frequently given. "In the days of Josiah the son of Amon, king of Judah, in the thirteenth year of his reign" (Jer. 1:2) God's word came to Jeremiah, and it came to Ezekiel in "the fifth year of the exile of King Jehoiachin" (Ezek. 1:2). In the Book af Haggai every oracle is dated by day and month: "In the second year of Darius the king, in the sixth month, on the first day of the month, the word of the Lord came by Haggai the prophet to Zerubbabel the son of Shealtiel, governor of Judah" (Hag. 1:1). Information about the dating of events is essential because we cannot understand the message unless we see it in relationship to the moment in history to which it is directed. The word that is given a date is usually directed toward the future. It leads Israel into the world of historical crises that come through the action of the Assyrian, neo-Babylonian, and Persian empires.

In keeping with this concern for dating, it is appropriate that we place the prophets in consistent chronological order, as the canon itself intended to do. In the era of the threats posed by the neo-Assyrian empire in the eighth century, Amos and Hosea appear in the northern kingdom, Isaiah in Jerusalem, and Micah in rural Judah. In the crisis brought about by the transition from the neo-Assyrian to the neo-Babylonian empire, in the second half of the seventh century, we find Nahum, Habakkuk, Zephaniah, and Jeremiah. The last of these continued his work after the collapse of Jerusalem in 587 B.C. After that catastrophe, Obadiah was active in Jerusalem; in the early decades of the Babylonian exile Ezekiel was active in Babylon, and around the middle of the sixth century, prior to the transition from the neo-Babylonian empire to the Persian Empire, Second Isaiah was active (Isa. 40–55). Zechariah experienced the return from exile and the new beginnings in Jerusalem. Together with Haggai he encouraged the rebuilding of the Temple in 521–520 B.C. There were also prophets active in Jerusalem at that time, whose messages were collected in Isaiah 56–66 (Third Isaiah). And during the crisis in the Persian Empire and the transition to the Hellenistic period in the fifth and fourth centuries, Malachi, Joel, Second Zechariah (9–11), Third Zechariah (12–14), and the author of the Isaiah Apocalypse (24–27) were active.

The Self-Understanding of the Prophet

How are we to explain the function of these men with a message? The prophets themselves make clear that their personalities are absorbed into Yahweh's activity in Israel. They explain the beginnings and the duration of their activity in those terms. Their confessions and the accounts of their calls bear witness to severe struggles with Yahweh; indeed, they were published in order to document the legitimacy of their mission and message in times when they were especially attacked and rejected. This can be seen clearly in Isaiah's autobiographical accounts that begin in 6:1 and continue through 8:18. From these and similar texts we can identify four chief elements of the prophetic self-understanding.

First, the great prophets are careful not to derive their message from their own desires and intentions. Not once did they take the initiative in seeking contact with Yahweh; he overwhelmed them when they least expected it. Amos described it by saying, "The lion has roared; who will not fear? The Lord God has spoken; who can but prophesy?" (3:8). When he was overcome by the vision of the devouring hordes of locusts and of consuming fire, in solidarity with his threatened people he appealed to God: "O Lord God, forgive, I beseech thee! How can Jacob stand? He is so small!" (7:2, 5). Jeremiah reports how he resisted: "I do not know how to speak, for I am only a youth" (1:6). Isaiah spoke of the hand that seized him and prevented him from accompanying his people on their way (8:11). All of them saw themselves confronted by an irresistible, compelling force.

Second, they did not become Yahweh's instruments in frenzy or ecstasy, but while fully conscious. They listened, observed, and answered. Thus, in contrast to all ecstatics, whose experience must always be reported by a third party, the prophets describe their own experiences. Isaiah heard a voice asking, "Whom shall I send, and who will go for us?" And in a free decision he responded, "Here am I! Send me" (6:8–9). When he was given the hard task of making the people unresponsive to God, he did not automatically accept it, but expressed his reluctance with the question, "How long, O Lord?" (6:11). Similarly to the way in which Amos was called to observe (Amos 7:8; 8:2), Jeremiah is asked in his visions, "Jeremiah, what do you see?" (1:11, 13). The prophets themselves must put into words what they have experienced. This is a primary indication that each one must bring to his task his individual gifts for seeing, testing, judging, and formulating. They are not depersonalized. Each one of them accepts responsibility.

Third, the breakthrough to what lies in the future is the heart of their mission and the essential element in their prophetic office. To be sure, they are concerned with Israel's traditions and history, and even more with its present, but the accounts of their calls and of the missions entrusted to them make it clear that the absolutely decisive factor is the announcing and bringing in of what is radically new. Thus the visions of Amos culminate in his seeing the coming end of Israel, from which there is no escape (Amos 8:1 f.; 9:1–4). The goal of Yahweh's commission is the destruction of cities and the devastation of the land (6:11). Jeremiah is assured that Yahweh's word determines the future (Jer. 1:11) and that the disaster from the north cannot be prevented (1:13 f.). The older prophets in their accusations presented the coming judgment as unavoidable and did not count on any improvement. Ezekiel too, at the start of his work, agreed (Ezek. 2:10). Only after the fall of Jerusalem did he seem to be entrusted with the work of a watchman and a warner (33:1–9; cf. 3:17–21), work that included the call to repentance (chap. 18; cf. Zech. 1:4). Then comes the unconditional promise of salvation in terms of resurrection from the death of exile (Ezek. 37), and the equally unconditional promise of return to the homeland (cf. Isa. 40:1–9). Down to the days of Malachi, Joel, and Third Zechariah, with many variations the constant message of prophecy is the God who is coming.

Fourth, no understanding of the figure of the prophet would be complete that failed to see him as a man under attack. As the one to whom God lays claim he is reluctant (Jer. 1:6–7) or terrified (Amos 3:8), and his resistance must be overcome (Ezek. 2:8). He is sent to obstinate rebels (Ezek. 2:3 ff.; 3:7 ff.; Isa. 30:9). His message brings him loneliness (Jer. 15–17) and persecution (Amos 7:10 ff.; Jer. 20:10; 36:1–32). His most shattering experiences, however, come from God. He must "wait for the Lord, who is hiding his face from the house of Jacob" (Isa. 8:17), because he is ridiculed on account of the threats he utters: "Let the purpose of the Holy One of Israel draw near, and let it come, that we may know it!" (Isa. 5:19). Jeremiah's lament is the most moving, "Wilt thou be to me like a deceitful brook, like waters that fail?" (15:18). "Thou art stronger than I, and thou hast prevailed. I have become a laughingstock all the day; everyone mocks me" (20:7). The prophets certainly did not have an unshaken confidence in their office and mission. Each of them was dependent on the fact of Yahweh's word repeatedly calling him into action (Jer. 15:19–21) and of Yahweh's power repeatedly filling him. (Mic. 3:8).

False Prophets

This dependency of the prophets on Yahweh is seen most clearly in their confrontations with "false prophets," who were a threat not only to the prophets but to their hearers as well. The false prophets cannot be distinguished by mannerisms or by an institution to which they belong. They can be recognized only in retrospect. Indeed, it is the old Greek translation that first introduced this distinction; the original text calls both the "false" and the "true" merely "prophets."

In reference to their relation to institutions, various categories of prophets can be distinguished. There were prophets such as

Nathan and Gad, who were connected to the royal court and gave advice to King David (2 Sam. 7, 12, 24). The groups of prophets around Ahab with Zedekiah son of Chenaanah and Micaiah son of Imlah are of this type (1 Kings 22:6–28). Isaiah also apparently had close relations to the court (Isa. 7), perhaps because of earlier activity as a teacher of traditional wisdom at the court school. There were also cultic prophets. Often prophets are mentioned alongside priests as comrades in the Temple (Isa. 28:7; Hos. 4:4 ff.; Jer. 26:7). They probably had the responsibility of bringing before Yahweh the laments of individuals and of the people, and then proclaiming either an answer or a rejection of the prayer (cf. Ps. 85:1–3, 8). Habakkuk probably was a cultic prophet, as the laments in 1:2–3, 12–13 show. Finally, we find free, individual prophets, such as Elijah and probably also the majority of the classic prophets whose prophecies are recorded. Amos is in sharp contrast to the high priest Amaziah of Bethel and to King Jeroboam (Amos 7:9–13). Isaiah and Jeremiah are contrasted to groups of priests and prophets (Isa. 28:7 ff.; Jer. 26:7 ff.). We must remember, however, that an institutional connection of one type or another is not decisive for the authority and truth of a prophetic proclamation. What is clear is that official connection with the court or the Temple can become a danger for the prophet.

The decisive factor is the prophet's relationship to Yahweh, which liberates him from the authority of those to whom he is sent. Being independent of his hearers is the inner seal of a true prophet. Micah says of the deceitful prophets that they "cry 'Peace' when they have something to eat, but declare war against him who puts nothing into their mouths" (Mic. 3:5). He saw himself as empowered by Yahweh's spirit to proclaim with power what is right, "to declare to Jacob his transgression and to Israel his sin" (3:8). A century later Jeremiah lamented, "They say continually to those who despise the word of the

Lord, 'It shall be well with you'; and to everyone who stubbornly follows his own heart, they say, 'No evil shall come upon you' " (Jer. 23:17). No one who had stood in Yahweh's council could have done that (23:22).

With this freedom from domination by one's hearers is connected the likelihood that when two prophets confront each other, the bringer of bad news is more likely to be on the side of truth than the bringer of good news. It is in this light that Jeremiah advises submission to Nebuchadnezzar (chap. 27) and opposes the prophet Hananiah (chap. 28) when the latter announces that Yahweh will break Nebuchadnezzar's yoke. Jeremiah quietly remarks that "the prophets who preceded you and me from ancient times prophesied war, famine, and pestilence" (28:7). A prophet who prophesies peace will be recognized as one whom Yahweh has sent only when his words come true (28:8–9). The prophetic tradition leads us to pay attention to a word of judgment and to be skeptical of a message of reassurance.

Jeremiah characterizes the false prophets by saying that "they commit adultery and walk in lies" (Jer. 23:14; 29:21–23). This corresponds to the ethical criteria of the Sermon on the Mount (Matt. 7:16). The life of the messenger reveals whether he is submissive to Yahweh's will or is following his own desires. The one who glorifies himself tries to manipulate the message.

Finally, only a true prophet can unmask a false one. That is a charismatic gift. The one who has stood in the council of Yahweh (Jer. 23:22) exposes the dreams and revelations of others as wishful thinking which comes out of the deceit in the human heart (Jer. 23:25–28). The true prophet may suffer defeat at the hands of a false one, but he rests his trust on the word of his God, and from that word draws new authority (Jer 28:11–16). He never gets the message from within himself

He may have to wait in despair for ten days, but he can do it (Jer. 42:7; cf. Isa. 8:17).

But how can those who hear the message distinguish between chaff and grain, between false prophet and true prophet? The hearer's eyes and ears are trained by observation of the confrontation between the two. With the help of the models in the material that has been handed down he is to test the independence of the prophet. Is the witness free from the domination of his hearers? Is he governed by his own wishes, or by the free will of his God? In suffering, the truth is convincingly documented. "My heart is broken within me, all my bones shake; I am like a drunken man, like a man overcome by wine, because of the Lord and because of his holy words" (Jer. 23:9).

EXCURSUS: *The Major Disciplines of Old Testament Studies*

At this point we can look briefly at the major disciplines of Old Testament studies. They all have the same central task—the explanation of the texts of the Old Testament.

Most significant in and for research and teaching is the continual interpretation of the biblical writings. Consequently, exegesis is and will remain the basis and goal of all other efforts in the field of Old Testament. Anyone who wishes to gain competence in exegesis would do well to begin with three of the more important books, one from each of the various types of Old Testament literature. From the Pentateuch, Genesis is the book usually chosen, though Exodus with its central theme of deliverance is equally well suited. For an encounter with the prophets, Isaiah, Jeremiah, and a selection from the Minor Prophets are to be recommended. And of course no one can afford to neglect the Psalms. In this way, the student, after gaining a general overview of the whole Old Testament by means of the standard "introductions," will be led methodically into the movement that gave rise to the separate texts, a movement that formed the basis for that faith in the midst of history which pointed the prophets to the future and which led to praise, lament, thanksgiving, and instruction for daily life.

The traditional comprehensive disciplines are the history of Israel, the literary history of the Old Testament (mistakenly called "introduction"), and Old Testament theology. Because the historical background of all the texts is so significant, a thorough study of Israel's history is desirable at an early stage. By contrast, a so-called introduction to the Old Testament writings as a whole should be studied only when the student, by work with individual books, has first practiced and learned to understand the methods of interpretation. Then an "introduction" can summarize and supplement the literary problems and results. Old Testament theology should have the same summarizing and supplementing function in reference to the theological structures and the message that is being proclaimed. Preparation for it should include a study of the major concepts of the Old Testament as they relate to the principles of speaking and writing in ancient Israel. Such concepts and principles, of course, are not to be ensconced within a theological system that is not based on the Old Testament itself. Old Testament theology cannot deny the historical character of the texts, and consequently today it is more and more determined in its outlines by Israel's history, but also and to no less a degree by the study of the literature of the Old Testament message, the form it took, and the manner in which it was preserved and handed on. Thus Old Testament theology proves to be a basic, normative history of the proclamation and can serve as the framework of biblical studies in any future study of theology.

Anyone who wants to do independent research in the Old Testament cannot ignore three related fields. The philology of the ancient Near East increases our understanding of the

Hebrew language and of the way the world was viewed. Because most Old Testament statements are intimately related to history, archaeology too is of the greatest interest. And comparative religion reveals similarities and differences between Israel's faith and that of the surrounding nations, and helps us recognize the distinctive nature of the history of proclamation in the Old Testament.

The purpose of all these comprehensive studies and all accompanying forms of special research remains the better understanding of the Old Testament books themselves. Exegesis remains the main task. Such books as Deuteronomy, Job, and Jonah increase one's delight in discovery and increase the expectation that still other parts of the Old Testament contain secrets which must not remain concealed.

THE LANGUAGE OF THE PROPHETS: FORM AND STYLE

The prophets were interested above all in pointing to Yahweh's future acts, and all the forms in which they cast their messages point to this goal. The close connections between acts and words show how completely this concern governed their work.

Symbolic Actions

The accounts of the symbolic actions of the prophets cast light on the use of prophetic language in general. The person of the prophet himself is a sign of Yahweh's activity. At the end of his early collection of messages Isaiah says, "Behold, I and the children whom the Lord has given me are signs and portents in Israel from the Lord of hosts, who dwells on Mount Zion" (Isa. 8:18). In concrete terms, Isaiah is saying something like this: When I took my son "A Remnant Shall Return" and went to meet King Ahaz to warn him against failing to trust Yahweh (7:2–9), and when later, because he rejected this warning, I named another son "The Spoil Speeds, the Prey Hastes" and set up in Jerusalem a tablet with this name written on it (8:1–4), then the God of Zion was present symbolically in my person and in the names of my children. I do not spread terror, but Yahweh himself is revealed in my activity as the one who terrorizes Israel (8:11–15). In Hos. 6:5 Yahweh says, "I have hewn them by the prophets, I have slain them by the words of my mouth." When Amos confronts Amaziah the priest at Bethel, then Amaziah is to know that in the prophet he is confronted by none other than Yahweh himself (Amos 7:14–16). Through these uninvited prophetic witnesses Yahweh was beginning a new activity in Israel.

Not only the person of the prophet but also the behavior of the prophet casts light on Yahweh's new intervention in the life of his people. The meaning of the names of Isaiah's children is a part of this. In a similar way, Hosea, with his whole family, is Yahweh's witness. His marriage with a prostitute illustrates the fact that in Israel nothing can be found except unfaithfulness to Yahweh (Hos. 1:2). Following this, the names of his children bear testimony that the blood shed at "Jezreel" will bring the downfall of Jehu's dynasty (1:4), that Yahweh will intervene "Without Pity" (1:6), and that Israel will be treated as if it is "Not My People" (1:9). These unusual names arouse expectancy. Jeremiah is to remain unmarried and childless, because there is no longer any future for mothers and children (Jer. 16:2 ff.). At other times prophets express hope for Israel by their actions. Hosea is to show love to an adulterous wife in order to portray Yahweh's love for his disloyal people (Hos. 3:1). During the hopeless days of the siege of Jerusalem, Jeremiah must buy a piece of land in order to give his personal seal to the expectation that "houses and fields and vineyards shall again be bought in this land" (Jer. 32:1–15). Thus the actions of the prophets present visually those actions of God that have been proclaimed and for which the people wait.

Finally, we find actions that are purely demonstrative. They illustrate a specific statement and impress on the memory with frightening clarity the reality of those acts of Yahweh that have been foretold. Among these is the setting up of the tablet in Isa. 8:1–2, which means that the city is legally transferred into the control of the Assyrians who are approaching at full speed in order to plunder it. On another occasion Isaiah shocked the city by walking through it naked and barefoot—disgraced like a prisoner of war—in order to portray the fate that awaited Egypt, in whose military might the people of Israel were still trusting. The shock of such acts keeps the message from being lost in the words; it becomes the talk of the town. And in addition, the symbolic action proclaims that the word will come true.

Speech

The prophetic signs are never transmitted without words to accompany them. The prophets never acted without speaking, and their speech demands our closest attention. No one else in ancient Israel explored the potentialities of speech as the prophets did. Let us look at a few of the stylistic forms they used.

How do the prophets put their statements together? Their public proclamations tend to be in poetry, though prose was also used. The remembrances in which they reported their commissioning, their visions, or symbolic actions generally do not display any poetic form. In other instances poetry has only subsidiary importance. Elevated prose is encountered more frequently than carefully wrought poetry. The metrical rules for ancient Hebrew verse have not yet been established with certainty. In addition, in the course of the transmission of the material differences have arisen that affect the syllable count. The clearest indication of a poetic style is the parallelism of the members, in which a relatively regular recurrence of lines and half lines occurs. The prophets used the antithetical parallelism that was a favorite of wisdom literature.

> Cease to do evil,
> Learn to do good.
>
> (Isa. 1:16*b*–17*a*)

The alternatives sharpen one's perception. More frequent is the use of synonymous parallelism, in which the repetition of meaning helps impress it on the memory.

> For I will be like a lion to Ephraim,
>   and like a young lion to the house of Judah.
> I, even I, will rend and go away,
>   I will carry off, and none shall rescue.
>
> (Hos. 5:14)

The meaning of one line is paralleled by that of the next. The relationship of the first and second lines to the third and fourth lines we call synthetic parallelism. The figurative language in the first two lines is explained in the next two. The last two lines contain the special form called climactic parallelism: the last line resumes the thought of the third line and carries it further. The form corresponds to the activity of Yahweh proclaimed here, with its stormy movement toward its goal.

A maximum of compression is achieved by the use of alliteration, especially in the conclusion of messages. Amos concludes the threat of exile for those who are sunk in immorality and luxury with the statement, "The debauchery of the dissolute shall die away" (Amos 6:7). Occasionally an end rhyme takes the place of alliteration, as in Hos. 8:7, "The grain dies before its hour; it yields no one any flour." Both these features are found in the untranslatable piling up of assonance at the climax of the artistic song of the vineyard in Isa. 5:7: "He expected them to do what is good, but instead they shed blood. He expected them to do what is right, but their victims cry in pain." Verses like this are written indelibly on the memory.

The same goal is achieved also by the use of figures of speech. We will take only two examples from the many that might be cited. The prophets had a particular fondness for metaphor, especially at the center of the message, where they were speaking of Yahweh and Israel. Hosea alone, in various passages, calls Yahweh Israel's husband, lover, fiancé, father, physician, shepherd, fowler, and even lion, leopard, bear, dew, fruit tree, moth, and dry rot. Hyperbole has even more impact, with its dramatic intensification which forces the hearer to recognize the verdict of guilty. A particularly effective choice of words is found in Amos 4:1, where he calls the rich women of Samaria "cows of Bashan," picturing the choice cattle being fattened for market, with their senseless trampling around (i.e., oppression), and their thirst for strong drink. His point of view is clear (cf. Isa. 5:22). Another effect is achieved by the use of irony. Amos took a catch phrase that expressed the confidence of his hearers that they would be saved and placed it in a new context: "As the shepherd rescues from the mouth of the lion two legs, or a piece of an ear, so shall the people of Israel who dwell in Samaria be rescued" (Amos 3:12). The comparison is ironic because Amos, on the basis of his life as a shepherd, cites the saving of a few fragments as proof of the total loss of the animal.

Biblical scholarship still has a long way to go in showing by means of the rich and diverse prophetic styles just what language can do. It goes without saying that the study must concern itself with the original text.

EXCURSUS: *The Methods of Textual Criticism*

Textual criticism is necessary if we are to come as close to the original text as possible. Some two thousand years of handing on the material in manuscript form provided for the possibility of many errors, and at times produced different forms of the text. All scholarly explanations of the text must begin with the attempt to determine the "original text."

The goal of textual criticism is the reconstruction of the text as it existed at the time when the biblical books took their final literary form prior to their canonization. The textual critic seeks to recognize and correct mistakes that occurred in the preparation, use, preservation, and copying of manuscripts. It is essential to distinguish the task of textual criticism from that of literary criticism (see above, pp. 35 ff.). This is best done in terms of their respective goals. Textual criticism seeks to establish the original wording of the completed biblical book, while literary criticism seeks to determine its preliterary history, the path that led from the first literary form of a text to the completion of the book as we now have it. In doing this the critic may discover various literary sources, as we saw in the consideration of the Pentateuch. He will endeavor to reconstruct these sources and to understand the manner in which the editor brought them together. Literary criticism has identified at least three sources in the book of the prophet Jeremiah. Along with the investigation of the history of the editing of the book goes the investigation of the possibility of later additions. For example, the identification of the oracles of salvation at the end of the Book of Amos (9:11–15) is a result of literary criticism, not textual criticism. In trying to establish the wording of the completed book, textual criticism assumes that there was more than one course followed in the transmission of the same original text. Textual criticism is also known as lower criticism; and literary criticism, with its concern for other questions, is also called higher criticism.

The materials for textual criticism need to be mentioned. The starting point is always the oldest available complete text of the Hebrew Old Testament. This is Manuscript B 19^A of the Public Library in Leningrad, which was copied about A.D. 1008. It can be compared with other medieval manuscripts and particularly with older Hebrew manuscripts preserved in fragmentary form. Among these the texts discovered in the caves on the northwest shore of the Dead Sea at Khirbet Qumran since 1948 are especially significant, because they date from the second and first centuries B.C. From the same period we have the Greek translation known as the Septuagint, the first five books of which date from the middle of the third century B.C.. The Septuagint takes its name from "the Seventy," a group of scholars who, according to the Letter of Aristeas, translated it. Back translation of it gives a text that can be compared with the Hebrew. A similar function is served by the Aramaic Targums, rather free paraphrases of the text which took their literary form somewhat later, and the Latin Vulgate, which is based largely on Hebrew texts of the fourth century A.D. Various other translations also provide opportunity for comparison with the Hebrew tradition.

The methods of textual criticism also deserve quick review. First of all, all available variant readings must be assembled. Then we try to determine how they arose. Even in the Masoretic tradition of the Hebrew scribes we must assume there were errors in copying and dogmatic corrections. For example, the ancient scribes specifically say that they "improved" the text of Gen. 18:22*b* that had come down to them, "But the Lord still stood before Abraham," so that it now reads in the Hebrew Bible, "But Abraham still stood before the Lord." Since the Hebrew word "stand" often means "serve," they considered the traditional text inappropriate. The context, however (cf. vv. 22*a* and 23*a*), indicates that the "unimproved" text is the original. In the investigation of the ancient translations we must reckon not only with scribal errors and dogmatic corrections but with linguistic difficulties, and with the necessity of transferring the material into another culture. In Hos. 2:7 the Septuagint translated the words "wool and flax" as "clothing and linen." The translation was prepared for the urban culture of Alexandria, which was more familiar with the finished products than with the raw materials of which Hosea had spoken in his rural environment.

After the variants have been examined, there are some basic rules that govern the choice among them. The shorter reading is usually preferred because, in the process of transmission, additions such as explanations and glosses are more probable than a shortening of the text, which would be prevented by respect for the text. For similar reasons the more difficult reading is generally preferred to a flat, easily intelligible one. The metrical form, in view of the uncertainties mentioned above (see p. 70), can serve only as a supplementary argument. Original attempts at improvement—conjectures—are a basic possibility in difficult cases. As a control on the material, we should always seek to explain how an erroneous reading might have arisen. We can take Amos 3:8 as an example. "The lion has roared; who will not fear? (The Lord) Yahweh has spoken; who can but prophesy?" In this case, "the Lord" can be recognized as an addition to the text, because in many passages the Septuagint presupposes only "Yahweh" where the Hebrew text has "the Lord Yahweh." So we can see that "the Lord" is a frequent addition. "Yahweh," as the shorter text, is the more probable reading. The meter can support this conclusion, since v. 8*b* has two half lines, each with two heavy beats, as does its parallel in 8*a*. So Amos here wrote two polished lines, each with two half lines in 2:2 meter. This view is supported by the later Jewish custom of avoiding the pronunciation of "Yahweh" and instead substituting "Lord," and also by the tendency to have a fuller-sounding designation of the deity. This example shows the significance that textual criticism has for the understanding of prophetic speech.

Literary Categories

The prophets drew on all areas of human life for their literary categories, only one of which can be singled out as being characteristic of prophecy, namely, the announcement. In form the announcement category has two characteristics: it is introduced by the formula, "Thus saith the Lord" (and sometimes concluded with "the Lord has spoken"), and Yahweh always speaks in the first person. This category belongs to the language of diplomacy in the ancient Near East; it is found in many letters from Mesopotamia. We also find it within the Old Testament, for example, in the report of Jephthah's dealings with the Ammonites in Judg. 11:12–17. The passage begins, "Then Jephthah sent messengers to the king of the Ammonites and said, 'What have you against me, that you have come to me to fight against my land?' " The sender of the message speaks in the first person. In vv. 14–15 we find the formula used for the beginning of the message, "And Jephthah sent messengers again to the king of the Ammonites and said to him, 'Thus says Jephthah. . . .' " There is a similar occurrence in Gen. 32:4–6. The prophets show that they are messengers of Yahweh when they make use of this category as the basic form of what they say. With their characteristic flexibility they were able to incorporate into this basic form many other categories. But before we look at the wealth of forms that they used we must examine the methods which scholarship has used, and will continue to use, to gain sharper insight into all areas of the Bible, especially the prophetic literature.

EXCURSUS: *Form Criticism*

The method known as form criticism investigates the fundamental elements of rhetorical and literary units, their context, and their function in the life of the people. It is an effort to get closer to the meaning of the individual statements and the significance of the larger units.

The method presupposes that specific categories of speaking or writing belong to specific occasions in life. In ancient times these categories had a fixed form. We saw how an unvarying basic form was used when a message was to be delivered. In similar manner, when there was a death in a family the category used was the lament, and at the conclusion of a legal process, the customary form was a verdict and the reasons for the verdict.

Form critical analysis of a passage leads to the identification of the structural elements of a discourse or a unit of text. It is important to recognize the syntactic form and the characteristic terms used. In the message, the formula "Thus has so-and-so spoken" is a fundamental element. In a hymn the imperative call to praise precedes the reason for or the content of the praise, in the indicative. In the acknowledgment of a lament "Fear not" is a typical term.

Form critical synthesis must look at the component parts in terms of the links that bind them together, especially the conjunctions. Only by looking at the totality of a category and comparing as many occurrences as possible can its function be seen. In the model of casuistic laws the case in question is introduced by "if," and the main clause then specifies the punishment. In a similar way the pronouncing of a sentence states the ground for the punishment, introduced with "because," and the punishment is introduced by "therefore." In times of public crisis, the call to the people to join in lamentation and fasting is accompanied by a statement of the reasons for the crisis—drought, pestilence, the threat of war. The importance of noting the key words can be shown in the comparison of a hymn with the call to public lamentation. Both combine an imperative with a statement of the reasons for the command. In the hymn we find, "Rejoice!" "Sing!" "Praise!" In the lament, "Howl!" "Mourn!" "Fast!" The difference of vocabulary demonstrates the totally different functions of the two forms.

This last example shows that the function of a category can be fully explained only when its sociological setting or *Sitz im Leben*, its "life setting," is recognized. For us today the relation of a passage to its ancient role in the life of the people is an indispensable commentary. Particularly for the study of the prophets, however, it is important to keep in mind the possibility that categories may move into new areas of life and become combined with other categories.

Life Settings

In the prophetic books we find categories from the most varied areas of life. This cannot be explained simply by saying that prophetic messages touch the whole of life, because the same can be said of the law codes and wisdom literature, which display a rather unified structure. We must also take into account the passionate concern of the prophets to make their messages heard, under the widest range of circumstances.

With comparative frequency categories are borrowed from the legal world. A principal form is the pronouncing of sentence, in which the statement of the sentence is combined with the reasons for it. The key word for this legal process is found in the beginning of Hos. 4:1–3: "The Lord has a controversy with the inhabitants of the land. There is no faithfulness or kindness, and no knowledge of God in the land; there is swearing, lying, killing, stealing, and committing adultery; they break all bounds and murder follows murder. Therefore the land mourns, and all who dwell in it languish." Prophets appear in the city gate, the courthouse of the Israelite cities, and on behalf of Yahweh take the roles of plaintiff and judge. "The Lord enters into judgment with the elders and princes of his

people: ' . . . What do you mean by crushing my people . . .?'
says the Lord God of hosts" (Isa. 3:14–15). The basic form of
the message can assume the category of accusation. In other
places it is more in the nature of a statement of the defense,
"Thus says the Lord: 'What wrong did your fathers find in me
that they went far from me?' " (Jer. 2:5).

Frequently we find categories that were used by the writers of
wisdom literature. Isaiah 28:23–29 is a didactic poem, which
begins with the typical call to pay attention to instruction, and
then in a series of rhetorical questions describes the various
activities and implements of a farmer, in order to conclude by
stating Yahweh's wise and marvelous plan as seen in his activity
in history. More often we encounter wisdom disputations, in
which the hearer is brought to make his own decision by means
of a flurry of questions which prepare the way for agreement
with the message. The message then is presented at the conclusion in the form of rhetorical questions or statements. Amos
3:3–6, 8 and Isa. 40:12–31 are illustrative in this regard. In
addition, the posing of a riddle, as in Ezekiel 17, is one of the
forms taken from wisdom literature.

Legal categories are used particularly where Israel's misdeeds
are under discussion, and forms from wisdom literature are
used where lack of insight is the enemy. The categories drawn
from cultic life are found primarily when the prophets are criti-
cizing the worship of the people. Amos, for instance, adopted
the form of priestly instruction for a pilgrimage and used it
ironically. " 'Come to Bethel, and transgress; to Gilgal, and mul-
tiply transgression; bring your sacrifices every morning, your
tithes every three days . . . proclaim freewill offerings, publish
them; for so you love to do, O people of Israel!' says the Lord
God" (Amos 4:4–5). In other passages the prophetic attack
takes the form of rejection of the cult (Amos 5:21–23; Isa.
1:11–15). Other prophets used cultic categories in their origi-

nal significance. Second Isaiah often expressed his proclamation of salvation in the form used for announcing that a petition has been answered, the key word being "Fear not!" (Isa. 41:10, 14; 43:1; also Lam. 3:57). He transformed the cultic hymn into an eschatological hymn (Isa. 42:10–13). Isaiah made use of the call for the people to lament in order to announce the imminent threat of war (Isa. 14:31)

The prophecies of doom make particular use of forms that belong to times of war, such as the call to take flight (Jer. 4:5 ff.) and the call to battle (Joel 4:9 ff.). The announcement of war, with the exhortation not to fear and the prediction of the defeat of the enemy, as in Isaiah's ultimatum to King Ahaz (Isa. 7:4–9), seems to make use of a traditional category (cf. Deut. 20:1–4).

There are also forms drawn from family life. The lament over the death of an individual becomes in the mouth of the prophet a dire warning of the expected downfall of the nation. "Fallen, no more to rise, is the virgin Israel; forsaken on her land, with none to raise her up" (Amos 5:2; cf. 5:16 f.). To express alienation the prophets used the complaint of a betrayed lover (Isa. 5:1–7) or the forms of divorce and marriage, from the marriage law (Hos. 2:4–22). The effect is quite striking. The various metaphors used of Yahweh led the prophets to make use of corresponding forms of speech.

When a small-town herdsman like Amos makes use of a typical form used in the royal court—the instructions given to a diplomat, as in Amos 3:9—we can take this as an indication of his freedom. Only a king gives instructions to his ambassadors in this way. "Proclaim to the strongholds in Assyria, and to the strongholds in the land of Egypt, and say, 'Assemble yourselves upon the mountains of Samaria.'" An international assembly, with power to judge, is called to witness the violence practiced in the Israelite capital. Amos adopted speech forms of the ruling classes in order to give expression to the authority of God's judgment.

Form critical explanation of the words of the prophets demonstrates the breadth, adaptability, and power of prophetic language. The prophets were able to adopt and transform categories from all areas of life, in order to proclaim their messages in a manner that is appropriate and cannot be ignored.

THE SOCIAL CRITICISM OF THE PROPHETS: SOCIETY, LAW, WORSHIP, POLITICS

The Locus and Function of Social Criticism

With the assistance of form critical analysis of the prophetic oracles, the locus and function of their social criticism can be easily identified, primarily in the prophetic words of judgment, and especially the announcements of punishment. This criticism serves as the ground for punishment. The diagnosis and the prognosis are usually closely connected; Yahweh's future execution of the sentence is shown to be the consequence of the guilt of those being addressed. Hosea's God says, "I will punish them for their ways, and requite them for their deeds" (Hos. 4:9*b*). The evil that has been brought to light is often described in a clause beginning with "because" (Hos. 4:1; Amos 5:11; Isa. 7:5), and Yahweh's threat of punishment is often added in a clause that begins with "therefore" (Hos. 4:3; Amos 5:12–17; Isa. 5:13).

Only rarely do we encounter criticism of society in independent sayings, in "woes" for example (Isa. 5:18–21), in parodies of priestly instruction (Amos 4:4–5), or in the song of a deceived lover (Isa. 5:1–7). Usually the use of such categories as these serves only to announce the divine judgment (Amos 6:1–7; Isa. 5:8–10; Amos 5:21–27). The close connection between accusations and denunciations remains typical of the prophetic criticism of society.

In addition it must be noted that the certainty that Yahweh is going to intervene to punish led the classical prophets of judgment to condemn the current behavior of their hearers. When the prophets tell of the tasks that Yahweh has committed to them, these tasks involve for the most part only the threat of judgment. In the actual statements the announcement of judgment is often given as a direct word from God, whereas the basis of guilt is indicated first in the prophet's own words (e.g., Amos 4:1–3; Isa. 5:8–10). In this way any doubts about God's justice are removed before they can be raised. As a consequence we cannot say that in prophecy the prognosis is the result of the diagnosis. The accounts of how messages were received from God and the structure of the messages themselves indicate just the opposite—it was the prophets' certainty of impending punishment that led them to recognize in their surrounding society the reasons for the punishment. In general, the sequence of stages by which the prophets gained their knowledge went from prognosis to diagnosis. In the proclamation, however, the diagnosis often was stated first.

Their certainty about the future came before their criticism of society, and this priority explains the lack of reforming or revolutionary traits in the words of the prophets. In the writings of the classical prophets there are very few exhortations (Amos 5:14–15; Isa. 1:16–17). In such exceptional cases, stress is laid less on a change in the circumstances than on a change of one's own behavior (Jer. 7:3–7). The conclusion "And you would not" (Isa. 30:9, 15; cf. Amos 4:6 ff.) is loud and clear. In general no improvement is expected from human beings. No program is drawn up for the future. In spite of the deep concern of the prophets for those who were oppressed, they were not their spokesmen. The prophets proclaim that God is judge, and their criticism of society is intended to demonstrate his righteousness.

They take a sober view of what humans can and cannot do. They do not excuse existing conditions; they announce their total transformation. This is what constitutes their greatness.

The Themes of Social Criticism

The themes of social criticism include all the significant areas of life. For example, the prophets attacked the society which no longer provided equal justice for all even though Yahweh had led all Israel together into freedom. Amos summarized as follows: "For three transgressions of Israel, and for four, I will not revoke the punishment; because they sell the righteous for silver, and the needy for a pair of shoes—they that trample the head of the poor into the dust of the earth, and turn aside the way of the afflicted; a man and his father go in to the same maiden" (Amos 2:6–7). Amos is condemning the practice of selling persons into slavery for debt. Innocent people lose their freedom, because children are laden with the debts of their dead father, or because the poor must sell their freedom for a minor debt. Might is ruthlessly enforced against right. Uninhibited lust dishonors defenseless young women. Amos sees the reason for Israel's fall in the fact that the greed of a few powerful men destroys the free institutions that should exist for all. "You trample upon the poor and take from him exactions of wheat" (Amos 5:11). Isaiah denounces the concentration of property in Jerusalem in the hands of a few. "Woe to those who join house to house, who add field to field, until there is no more room, and you are made to dwell alone in the midst of the land" (Isa. 5:8; cf. Mic. 2:1 ff.). Just as Amos accused the leading circles in Samaria of piling up wealth in their palaces by means of force and oppression (Amos 3:9 f.), so Jeremiah condemned King Jehoiakim for plundering the fruits of his people's toil; he "makes his neighbor serve him for nothing, and does not give him his wages," in order to be able to build "a great house with spacious upper rooms . . . paneling it with cedar, and painting it with vermilion" (Jer. 22:13*b*–14).

Society is also corrupted by dishonesty. Amos denounced the commercial practices which deceived the buyer by crooked scales, inferior wares, and exorbitant prices (Amos 8:4–6). The ruling class wallowed in luxury at the expense of those they were exploiting. They held noisy feasts (Amos 6:1–3, 6; 4:1 f.) and lived in pretentious idleness (Isa. 3:16 ff.; cf. 5:11–12, 22). Thus a large number of the abuses in an early capitalistic society were exposed. In questions of property, the poorest person becomes the standard by which a society is measured.

At the heart of the complaints is the fact that no one can be sure of receiving justice. Unequal distribution of wealth and unequal justice reinforce each other. Judges "take a bribe, and turn aside the needy in the gate" (Amos 5:12). "Every one loves a bribe and runs after gifts. They do not defend the fatherless, and the widow's cause does not come to them" (Isa. 1:23). The city gate, as the largest open area in the city, served as the place where cases were tried. Amos had listened to what went on there, and he had come to a conclusion about it. "O you who turn justice to wormwood, and cast down righteousness to the earth! . . . They hate him who reproves in the gate, and they abhor him who speaks the truth" (Amos 5:7, 10). And Isaiah saw that the perversion of justice was bringing disaster on Israel. "Woe to those who call evil good and good evil, who put darkness for light and light for darkness" (Isa. 5:20). Wherever right and justice perish, the social structures that should promote welfare crumble and the sources of life dry up (Amos 5:24; 6:12; Isa. 5:7). In matters of justice, the highest sensitivity is called for.

The people of Israel should know this through their worship. The value of true worship is beyond estimate, as the source of power and direction for all of life, as the place where the sick receive healing and those who have fallen are raised up again.

But the place where people should receive healing from Yahweh has been turned into a carnival of human activity. In Amos's opinion, the pilgrimages to Bethel and Gilgal served to increase the lust for crime (Amos 4:4–5). The only motive for bringing sacrifices and gifts was self-love. And so the prophet announced Yahweh's sharp rejection of it all: "I hate, I despise your feasts, and I take no delight in your solemn assemblies. Even though you offer me your burnt offerings and cereal offerings, I will not accept them, and the peace offerings of your fatted beasts I will not look upon. Take away from me the noise of your songs; to the melody of your harps I will not listen. But let justice roll down like waters, and righteousness like an everflowing stream" (Amos 5:21–24). In similar terms Isaiah portrayed cultic activity as an attempt at self-gratification. In true worship, Yahweh wants to be known as the one who helps the oppressed and secures the rights of widows and orphans (Isa. 1:10–17). Hosea expressed Yahweh's will in terms of a sharp antithesis: "I desire steadfast love and not sacrifice, the knowledge of God, rather than burnt offerings" (Hos. 6:6). Down to the postexilic period this emphasis was maintained in the messages of the prophets. The preacher whose words are contained in Isaiah 58 distinguished between the fasts that Israel was keeping and those that please Yahweh. Israel was observing fasts in which a man would "bow down his head like a rush, and . . . spread sackcloth and ashes under him" (Isa. 58:5). Yahweh, however, was looking for a day of penitence. "Is not this the fast that I choose: to loose the bonds of wickedness, to undo the thongs of the yoke, to let the oppressed go free, and to break every yoke? . . . to share your bread with the hungry, and bring the homeless poor into your house; when you see the naked, to cover him, and not to hide yourself from your own flesh?" (Isa. 58:6–7).

There can even come a time in which a prophet like Haggai can reprimand selfish people who are concerned only with their own houses, and remind them that Yahweh's Temple lies in ruins, and that because they neglect to honor Yahweh, they are no longer able to find a way out of their troubles (Hag. 1:2 ff.). Concrete efforts for the sanctuary make it evident who it is from whom Israel is expecting salvation (2:4–9). In the name of Yahweh, Malachi can rebuke people for offering in the Temple sick and lame animals that they would not dare to offer to their governor (Mal. 1:8 ff.). The Temple is no place for discarding things for which you have no use. In all ages, worship makes clear the source from which Israel expects the gift of life. Contemptuous worship is just as much to be rejected as self-interested worship.

The aberrations in worship work themselves out also in politics. A good example is found in the messages relating to the Syro-Ephraimite War (733 B.C.). These messages have been preserved from both sides of the battle lines—from the northern kingdom in the words of Hosea, and from Jerusalem in the words of Isaiah. After the collapse of the anti-Assyrian coalition, Hosea condemned the policy by which "Ephraim went to Assyria, and sent to the great king," because "he is not able to cure you or heal your wound" (Hos. 5:13). The superpower will only swallow Ephraim up, making it useless in the midst of the nations (8:7–9). The payment of exorbitant tribute buys only wind; Ephraim remains unstable (12:2). A hopeless and vacillating international policy that trusts first in Assyria and then in Egypt (7:11 f.) corresponds to the internal revolts against the throne, which come about because no one asks what Yahweh's will is (8:4). In politics too there is no salvation as long as Israel worships as its god the work of its own hands (14:3).

At the climax of the Syro-Ephraimite War Isaiah encountered King Ahaz of Judah as Jerusalem was being threatened by the allied Arameans and Israelites. Ahaz was worrying about how to defend the city, but Isaiah said to him, "Do not fear." Yahweh was at work to defeat their enemies. "If you do not believe, surely you shall not be established" (Isa. 7:4–9). Isaiah also warned against a foreign policy based on alliances that paid more attention to human cleverness and power than to Yahweh's wisdom and his sovereign and decisive power (cf. 31:1–3).

Prophetic criticism of politics assumes that Yahweh is sovereign over the foreign nations also. Long series of oracles about the nations confirm this. The nations that surrounded Israel, both great and small, were subject to Yahweh's will. In the ancient wars that Yahweh had fought on behalf of his people, the belief had been proclaimed that Yahweh could control all their enemies. Amos, then, invited the enemies to judge Israel (Amos 6:14; 3:11). Isaiah portrayed vividly the superiority of Yahweh as master of the Assyrian empire. He will whistle for them to come like bees (Isa. 7:18 f.), shave with them like a razor (7:20), use them like a saw, and swing them like an ax (10:15). Jeremiah called Nebuchadnezzar Yahweh's "servant" (Jer. 27:6), and Second Isaiah called Cyrus Yahweh's "anointed" (Isa. 45:1). Israel is not to suppose that the unrest of world politics will result in anything except the carrying out of the plans of Israel's God (Isa. 14:26).

The foreign nations, if they misunderstand their limited task as God's instruments and self-confidently carry through their own plans of subjugation and extermination, are not exempt from the judgment that Yahweh brings to bear on Israel (Isa. 10:5 ff., 13 ff.). "Shall the axe vaunt itself over him who hews with it?" (Isa. 10:15a). It is not only arrogant world powers like Assyria that are subject to this judgment, but a little country like Edom as well. If Edom takes malicious and unbrotherly delight in the conquest of Jerusalem (Obad. 11 ff.), that too is a form of arrogance (Obad. 3), and the prophets denounce it as a violation of the conditions of international relations. Just as individuals in Israel must behave toward one another in civilized ways, so must the nations behave in their relations with each other. Amos himself condemned not only the cruelty of Israel's neighbors toward Israel but also the cruelties of the nations toward each other (Amos 2:1 f.).

The Themes of Prophetic Proclamation

The comprehensive social criticism of the prophets leads us to try to identify the main themes of their proclamation. The first is Yahweh's uniqueness as the sovereign Lord of all nations and all areas of life. Even in his messages about the foreign nations, Amos does not mention any other gods (Amos 1:3–2:3; 9:7). Second Isaiah expressed what all the others presupposed, that it is Yahweh and he alone who directs history (Isa. 43:10–13). As a nation that bears witness to the only Lord, Israel is subject to the most severe judgment (Amos 3:2).

This is because Israel has experienced God's blessings and benefits. How can Israel look to any other power for deliverance, when it has experienced Yahweh's liberating rule ever since the exodus from Egypt and the occupation of the promised land (Hos. 11:1–7; 13:4 ff.; Jer. 2:18 ff.; Ezek. 20)? And following God's choice of Zion, Israel has experienced Yahweh's unfailing presence and support (Isa. 28:14–16; 31:4 ff.; Zech. 12:2 ff.). In the midst of its perverse political life, Israel is reminded of Yahweh's saving deeds.

Knowledge of God demands reliability and faithfulness (Hos. 4:1 f.; Amos 2:6–9). Worship in Israel should remind the people of all that Yahweh has done and make his word a present reality to guide their way (Hos. 4:4–6). His word includes the righteous teachings and laws which he has given them (Hos. 8:12; 6:6). The people were expected to produce the fruits of justice and righteousness (Isa. 5:1–7; Amos

5:24). Jeremiah reminded King Jehoiakim of what his father King Josiah had done: "Did not your father eat and drink and do justice and righteousness? . . . Is not this to know me?" (Jer. 22:15–16). The motivation of the prophets' social criticism is to be found in the knowledge of God, of which Israel had failed to make use. When people who have been liberated and richly blessed no longer remember the one who has freed them and taught them to do right, then they oppress and plunder others because they desire to liberate and enrich themselves. Human society collapses if God is forgotten. Autonomous man attains at best a reversal of the roles of oppressor and oppressed, but he can never do away with oppression as such. In their message the prophets gave concrete expression to this truth.

THE EXPECTATIONS OF THE PROPHETS: FROM AMOS TO SECOND ISAIAH

While the prophetic word was related to the current scene, we must not lose sight of the fact that it was also deeply rooted in ancient Israelite traditions. How often the prophets reminded their hearers of the exodus from Egypt, of Yahweh's gift of the promised land, of the wilderness wanderings, of the covenant, and also of Jacob and David; later they called attention to Noah as well and to creation. They saw their contemporaries in a broad context, not only that of the surrounding nations and the crises of world history that were about to break over them, but also that of their own history, especially their beginnings. This lets us measure the wide range of prophetic proclamation. Remembrance of the past, however, was not a matter of independent interest to the prophets. It was connected rather with the current situation, because the traditions cast light either on the present guilt of Israel or on the immediate future—and the announcement of coming events was the prophets' main task.

It is difficult, even dangerous, to reduce the prophets' message about the future to a single formula. Since similar expressions are repeated from Amos to Malachi, Yahweh's intervention could be cited as the general theme, but the meaning and alarming nature of this intervention must first be discerned in more concrete terms. Three factors help to determine it: the current situation of the hearers, the various ancient traditions of Israel, and the current historical situation of the nations of the world. Since what the prophets said about the future changed with the changing course of world history, we can observe the several changes in the message. Let us look at them in chronological order.

Amos

Amos, as the earliest of the classic prophets, presents us with a typical example of the message concerning the one who is coming. According to his own account, his message is the result of visions and auditory experiences; it was not arrived at by an analysis of the situation in Israel or by observation of developments in the surrounding nations (7:1–8; 8:1 f.; 9:1–4; 7:14 f.; 3:8). The basic content of all that Amos said was determined by what Yahweh said to him in rare moments. Yahweh himself was coming to judge Israel, and there was no way to escape him (9:1–4; 2:13–16; 5:16–20). That he "will never again pass by them" means that Israel's end is near (7:8; 8:2; 5:1–3). This is the theme of the message concerning the future. As Amos proclaimed it, it was characterized by the three points of reference already mentioned. The unjust relationships of that day were the basis for Yahweh's intervention to administer righteous punishment (2:6–8; 5:12; 6:1, 3–6). The remembrance of Yahweh's fundamental act of intervention in Israel's early history made it clear that at present Israel had fallen away from God, who takes the side of the weak against the strong (2:9); it also was the basis of Yahweh's right to discontinue the special relationship which he had entered into when he chose this rebellious nation of Israel (3:2). It is against the background of God's gift of the land, a gift that was basic to Israel's history as a nation, that we must view the threat of a conquest of the land and deportation of the people (5:3, 5, 27; 4:2 f.; 6:7; 7:11, 17). Only when we see the approaching catastrophe as the end of salvation history do we become aware of its full significance. To this extent Amos's proclamation can be termed eschatological. Amos did not give a description of the setting in terms of world history, but he did indicate the setting when he spoke of the "adversary" who would surround the land (3:11), or of the "nation" that would oppress Israel from one end of the country to the other (6:14). The troubles that were arising in the world of international affairs were caused by none other than Yahweh himself. The prophet was expecting a future that would bring a totally new act of Yahweh, the termination of Israel's history as it had been up to that time. Outside of the death of Israel, Amos did not foresee anything of significance in the offing.

Hosea

Already for Hosea things were different. To be sure, he too knew that the previous salvation history was coming to an inevitable end. He cited Israel's apostasy from Yahweh to the Baals as the reason why Yahweh was taking away the blessings of a settled society. Israel, the wanton wife, "did not know that it was I who gave her the grain, the wine, and the oil. . . . Therefore I will take back my grain in its time, and my wine in its season" (2:8–9). Hosea spoke of the end of the history of God's people as it had been to that time; he portrayed the coming punishment with great clarity when he negated the old relationship and turned the covenant formula into a divorce formula, "You are not my people, and I am not your God" (1:9). The approaching doom in world history is made clearer in Hosea than in Amos, because Assyria is specifically named. The deportation of the people to Assyria will undo the exodus from Egypt. "They shall not remain in the land of the Lord; but Ephraim shall return to Egypt, and they shall eat unclean food in Assyria" (9:3; cf. 11:5; 8:13). The similarity to the message of Amos is clear.

What is new, first of all, is the way that Yahweh, in Hosea's proclamation, has to struggle to bring himself to such harsh verdicts. "What shall I do with you, O Ephraim? What shall I do with you, O Judah?" (6:4). Yes, Yahweh suffers unspeakably because all the punishments he has meted out and even the reversal of the exodus itself are not adequate to bring Israel back from its rebellion against him (11:1-7). The obstinacy of dying Israel is answered by warm compassion. "How can I give you up, O Ephraim! How can I hand you over, O Israel! . . . My heart recoils within me, my compassion grows warm and tender. I will not execute my fierce anger, I will not again destroy Ephraim; for I am God and not man, the Holy One in your midst, and I will not come to destroy" (11:8-9). Would it be possible to express with more passion the fact that Yahweh himself cannot bear to surrender Israel? There is no sign in Israel of a turn for the better. Israel remains blind to Yahweh, seeking help first from the gods of Canaan, then from political powers, but even so Yahweh's compassion breaks through as the sole ground for a new beginning beyond the impending end. "They shall come trembling like birds from Egypt, and like doves from the land of Assyria" (11:11). In another passage the restoration is based on the promise, "I will heal their faithlessness; I will love them freely" (14:5). In the shelter of

God's supreme love a new life will begin (14:6–9). This testimony to Yahweh's change of heart probably dates from the time when Hosea had already seen warfare devastate Israel's cities after the invasion of Tiglath-pileser III (11:6), events that were still far in the future in Amos's day. Even in Hosea's early pronouncements of judgment Yahweh expressed the hope that taking the people of Israel back into the wilderness would lead them to return to their "first husband," and so bring about a renewal of salvation history (2:6–7, 14–15; 3:4–5). Beyond the end, Hosea expected that Yahweh would make a new beginning with Israel, a beginning which would be the result of Yahweh's future work.

Isaiah

This hope was developed much more fully by Isaiah and the circle of his followers, but even then it would be realized only after a great impending judgment. The history of Yahweh's love for Israel, based on faithfulness to the covenant and on justice, ends in injustice and cries of distress (5:1–7; cf. 1:2–3). The new element, lacking in Amos and Hosea, who worked in the northern kingdom, is the manner in which Isaiah reminds Jerusalem of the history of David. It was a time of unparalleled prosperity, with victory over the Philistines on Mount Perazim and in the valley of Gibeon, and with the conquest of Jerusalem (2 Sam. 5:6–9, 17–25). Now the city must reckon with the fact that its time of glory is changed into its exact opposite. "For the Lord will rise up as on Mount Perazim, he will be wroth as in the valley of Gibeon; to do his deed—strange is his deed! and to work his work—alien is his work!" (Isa. 28:21). Yahweh, who secured victory for Israel in David's holy wars against the Philistines, is now fighting a holy war against Israel. In contrast to Yahweh's "proper work" in previous history, this is his "strange work." As David once besieged the Jebusite city of Jerusalem, so Yahweh himself will now besiege the Israelite city of Jerusalem and destroy it (29:1 ff.).

Isaiah portrayed Assyria as the tool of judgment much more clearly than Hosea had done. Isaiah sees the Assyrian troops approach in swift marches (5:26–30); they pitch their camps in the ravines of the Judean mountains (7:19), and overrun Jerusalem (8:7 f.). He hears the barbaric language of the conquerors (18:11, 13), and he foresees their plundering and robbery (10:6). But he also sees how Yahweh turns against his instrument, since Assyria had pursued its own ambitious plans and not observed the limits set by Yahweh (10:7 ff.). From the beginning Isaiah probably had in mind the limits of Yahweh's judgment. The name of his oldest son hints at this, "A Remnant Shall Return" (7:3; cf. 1:8 f.). In other passages Isaiah showed the function of Yahweh's intervention. Zion, the city whose leaders had become misleaders, and whose officials lived by bribery, was to feel Yahweh's wrath like a fire in which all dross would be purged away (1:21–25). The catastrophe in salvation history would bring purification: "And I will restore your judges as at the first, and your counselors as at the beginning. Afterward you shall be called the city of righteousness, the faithful city" (1:26). Just as Hosea foresaw a renewal of the gift of the land (Hos. 2:18; 11:11), so Isaiah foresaw the return of Jerusalem's best days. The early period had become a type of the period of the end.

Hosea based the new time of prosperity on Yahweh's unrequited love. Isaiah appreciably broadened the expectation of what would happen beyond the time of judgment and made it greater than the corresponding early period. He (or his pupils, as some scholars believe) did this in two respects. First, he extended the duration of this period for Israel. When Yahweh brings his people through the dark time of the Assyrian crisis and leads them to a new light, then he will install a new David as prince of peace and so begin a new era of prosperity without end (9:1–6). Here the Nathan oracle (2 Sam. 7:16), through the judgment on the previous kings of the Davidic dynasty (cf. Isa. 11:1 ff.; Mic. 5:1 ff.), has become an eschatological, messianic expectation. This eschatology no longer means only the end of what has been in existence; it means something of permanent validity. Second, the scope of the expectation is extended. Isaiah 2:2–4 includes the many different nations in the peace which will flow from Zion by Yahweh's word. The nations will go to the place where Yahweh reveals himself, and in obedience to his commands beat their weapons into peaceful implements. Thus Isaiah expands Israel's hope by giving it final validity and universal scope.

Jeremiah

Jeremiah's future expectation was similar to that of Hosea. At the beginning of his career under King Josiah about 627 B.C. Jeremiah spoke rather generally about a foe out of the north (1:14; 4:6). Later he described conquest at the hands of Nebuchadnezzar as unavoidable (27:6). But for Jeremiah too the judgment was a transition to a new life by Yahweh's grace and compassion. "The people who survived the sword found grace in the wilderness" (31:2). During Nebuchadnezzar's siege of Jerusalem, Jeremiah, although deprived of his freedom, purchased a plot of land belonging to a relative in order to demonstrate by his action that "houses and fields and vineyards shall again be bought in this land" (31:1–15). In the midst of the catastrophe he saw the reality of the future. Did he expect only a return to previous conditions? In the materials that have come down to us under his name we find for the first time the key word "new" used to designate the future: "Behold, the days are coming, says the Lord, when I will make a new covenant with the house of Israel and the house of Judah" (31:31). In what does the new consist? Hosea's message of God's healing of the people who were unable to repent (Hos. 14:5; cf. Jer. 3:22 ff.) was here made specific in three aspects. First, God's will will be written on Israel's heart; that is to say, as they are taught, they also receive the willingness and capacity to obey (Jer. 31:33). Second, there is no longer any need for anyone to teach anyone else, because all will be in a direct relationship to Yahweh (31:34a). Finally and above all, the removal of all guilt becomes the basis of a new covenant that cannot be broken (31:34b). That is Jeremiah's message of things with final validity, but it is not given universal application.

Ezekiel

Ezekiel made his appearance in 593 B.C. in Babylon among the exiles who belonged to the first group that had been deported in 597. His writings give us the most precise indications of how the proclamation of God's judgment on Jerusalem was transformed into the expectation of salvation, once the city had been destroyed. First he had to put an end to all false hopes. Jerusalem must taste the bitter dregs of its downfall, through fire, the sword, and the scattering of the survivors (5:1 ff.). Israel was to experience even the destruction of the Temple, without raising a single voice in mourning (24:15 ff.). But after the prophet heard the news that the city had fallen, his mouth was opened for the proclamation of a new message (24:25–27; 33:21 f.) which was expressed in many and varied ways during the next fifteen years. We will look at only two instances, the first being the message of the new life given to dry bones. The message came to people who, in total despair after the catastrophe, were saying, "Our hope is lost; we are clean cut off" (37:11). There was no attempt to pretty things up—nothing is left but scattered bones and graves. But the breath of life from God's spirit, which begins to blow as the prophet speaks, will bring new life to those who have died without hope, will lead them home and give them full knowledge of Yahweh (37:1–14). The focus in this instance is on the whole nation that has met its end, but in other messages Ezekiel turned his attention to the individual Israelite. Here too he spoke of the new covenant relationship that was to be awaited (36:28). The covenant itself is not termed "new," but Ezekiel speaks of a "new heart" and a "new spirit" as Yahweh's free, unconditional gifts (11:19; 36:26). The nations too are to come to a knowledge of Yahweh (36:21–22, 36). In 18:31 we are startled to find the exhortation, "Get yourselves a new heart and a new spirit! Why will you die, O house of Israel?" This extends the offer so that every generation, and every individual at every stage of his life, may turn back to Yahweh, who is ready to give everyone life and not death (18:1 ff.). The message of salvation has its effect in the present situation of lost and despairing men.

Second Isaiah

In Second Isaiah, "new" becomes the theological motto of the message about what is coming. The prophet was addressing the second generation of exiles, probably between 550 and 540 B.C. Among them the view was widespread that Yahweh had not only forsaken and forgotten Zion but was incapable of restoring it again (40:27; 49:14). In the face of this despair the prophet announced that the end of the exile was near, that Yahweh himself would lead his people like a shepherd and take them home by the road he had prepared, and that Cyrus would be Yahweh's instrument, Zion rebuilt, and the glory of Yahweh revealed in the sight of all the nations (40:1–11; 44:24–45:6; 52:7–12). The prophet did not answer skepticism with mere appeals, but with clear concepts and with cogent arguments.

Not only did he begin by introducing the concept "future" in relation to what he was proclaiming (41:22 f.), he also designated what the future would bring in its entirety as "new," to be distinguished from the "earlier things" (42:9 f.). Formerly it was completely unknown (48:6), and because of it the past can be forgotten (43:18 f.). The new exodus will be totally different from the first—it will be full of rejoicing and peace (52:12; 55:12 f.). The nations will line both sides of the road and discover God's glory and the power of his arm (40:4; 52:10).

What arguments did Second Isaiah offer those who pointed to Yahweh's apparent lack of power? First and most important he showed that the situation of the exile was entirely the result of the messages that Yahweh had spoken beforehand (41:21–24; 43:8–13). Their desperate situation was shown to be the fulfillment of the prophetic word—and as such a ground for trusting in the new prophetic word (41:25 ff.; 42:9; 55:10 f.). In addition, the prophet pointed to Abraham and Sarah, and so to the miracle by which God created something in a situation that was without hope (41:8 f.; 51:1 ff.). Finally, all of creation serves as a witness that there are no limits to what God can do (40:12–31; 45:11–13; 48:12–15). God's new intervention is shown to be a revelation of his universal saving glory and his proven power.

The disciples of this prophet of the exile consequently spoke of the expectation of "new heavens and a new earth" (65:17; 66:22). At the same time, however, the course of events led to new disappointments and to discouragement. In the writings of the postexilic prophets the hope was reduced and restricted, yes, even altered. Over the centuries Israel had to learn through the song of an unknown author (Isa. 52:13–53:12) that God's servant is one who, though despised and avoided by others, takes the sorrow and failure of many on himself so that they may have peace and healing, and so that all those among the nations who despise him will be astonished and put to silence, won over to him, and with him be saved to partake of a new life. Thus the future expectations of the Old Testament prophets offer models of fear and hope for the people of the New Testament on their tortuous paths from the cross of Jesus to a new world.

EXCURSUS: *The Social Structure of Ancient Israel*

Study of the social criticism of the prophets and of their eschatology presupposes a knowledge of the forms of community life in Israel. The Jerusalem of the future is to have new judges and counselors (Isa. 1:26). Second Isaiah's disciples said, "As a young man marries a virgin, so shall your builders marry you" (Isa. 62:5). What concepts of social life underlie examples like this?

Marriage, the smallest unit of society, is established by law, according to which the suitor gains his beloved by payment of the bride price to her father (Exod. 22:15 f.; cf. Hos. 2:21 f.). Monogamy, based on personal choice of one's mate, was the predominant form in Old Testament times (1 Sam. 18:20). Secondary wives, chosen from among slaves, were a possibility for assuring descendants (Gen. 16:1 f.). Having more than one wife had social and political significance, but in the case of Solomon it was condemned as apostasy from Yahweh (1 Kings 11:1 ff.).

The extended family was patriarchal in nature; the existence of matriarchy is difficult to establish. Married sons and their families belonged to the "house," the head of which was the "father." This family unit was preserved in the transition from a seminomadic life to a settled life; in the militia, the "house," as an extended family, counted as a unit of "fifty" (1 Sam. 8:12).

The next larger unit was the clan, which constituted a geographic community and provided a unit of a "thousand" for the militia. It was directed by a group of "elders," who were responsible for the dispensing of justice at the city gate (1 Kings 21:8).

A group of clans composed a tribe. The king whose coming is promised in Mic. 5:1 comes from the tribe of Judah, from the "thousand" that had settled in Bethlehem and as a clan bore the name "Ephrathah," and from the extended family of Jesse (Isa. 11:1), the father of David. The leader of the tribe was its spokesman in the Israelite tribal league (Exod. 22:27; Num. 31:13; 32:2). At the head of the league was probably the "judge," the one who rendered legal decisions (Judg. 10:1–5; 12:7–15). Later his position in the state was taken over by the king, with his officials, military commanders, judges, counselors, and priests. The postexilic community was led by the high priest (Hag. 1:1) and a council of elders (Joel 1:2), in addition to the governor appointed by the foreign empire that ruled them.

3. The Present: The Books of Teaching

PRAISE AND LAMENT: PSALMS AND SONGS OF LAMENT

We come now to the "Writings," those books that form the third and youngest part of the Hebrew canon. The Greek translation of the Bible removed Chronicles, Ezra, and Nehemiah from the Writings and placed them with the older works of history. Luther gave to the major part of the remaining books the title "Books of Teaching." The Greek Bible took them from the end of the canon and placed them in the middle, between the historical books and the prophecies. This arrangement made sense, because the Writings were intended to cast light on the present life, as one goes from past history with its testimonies to the future which the prophets foretold. Wisdom teachings, poetry, and prayers are offered as a means of answering or at least living with the most pressing questions of life and the question of God.

The chief place among the Books of Teaching is given to the Psalter, because it is through conversation with Yahweh that man achieves reason. The most common psalm categories are the songs of praise and songs of lament. Praise is chiefly an echo of the experience of Yahweh's saving deeds, and lament expresses hope that God will come to us.

Songs of Praise

Praise and lament are also found outside the Psalter. There the life setting of the songs can be discovered in the context of the stories, whereas in the song collections themselves—the Psalter and the little book of Lamentations—the *Sitz im Leben* can be discovered only indirectly. The setting of the songs is often indicated in the psalm "titles," but these are for the most part late additions.

We have already looked at the song of Miriam in Exod. 15:21 as a direct response to the liberation of the persecuted people from the power of the Egyptians (cf. Exod. 14). The song of Moses, which now precedes it in Exod. 15:1–18, has borrowed much of its language, but goes much further in its poetic reconstruction of the events and in its theological reflections. The song of Moses brings in also the events of the conquest of Canaan; their climax, for the singer, is the construction of the Temple sanctuary on Zion. In this way the spontaneous song of victory was expanded during the course of centuries to become a hymn.

The song of Deborah in Judges 5 is, according to its content and the narrative context, the result of direct divine assistance in a time of great trouble. In 1 Sam. 2:1–10 we find in the psalm of Hannah a song of thanksgiving to God for answering her prayer for a son (1:11 f., 19 ff.). One of David's songs of thanksgiving is directly related to an earlier plight in which he had found himself (2 Sam. 22:7; cf. Ps. 18). In addition to the hymns of Israel, which sing Yahweh's basic saving deeds, there developed the individual's song of thanks in response to the answering of specific petitions. Petitions were expressed in the category of songs of lament, in which people brought before Yahweh their various troubles—the childlessness of Hannah, the threats that David's enemies posed for him, the sickness of King Hezekiah (2 Kings 20:2 f.)—and prayed for deliverance from them. Hezekiah's prayer shows us that insistence on one's innocence (2 Kings 20:3) formed an element in such laments, and Hannah's prayer shows us a vow (1 Sam. 1:12) as another element. Later the boundaries between the categories were no longer so distinct. In Jonah 2, a song of thanksgiving was used as a prayer of lamentation in a situation of great distress. In Isaiah 12; Amos 4:13; 5:8 f.; 9:5 f., and other passages the community uses a hymn as a response to the prophetic word. In other places the prophets themselves use hymnic elements (Isa. 42:10 ff.) or laments (Jer. 8:18; 10:19 f.) to convey their messages. The books of Chronicles show how in the fourth century psalms were brought together for use in worship, as we can see in 1 Chronicles 16, which is made up from Psalms 105, 96, and 106.

Growth of the Psalter

The collecting of psalms into a Psalter must have had its beginning already by this period. In its completed form the collection was called *Tehillim*, that is, "Praises." As a collection, it was intended primarily for use in praising Yahweh. This is confirmed also by the present division into five "books," a structural feature perhaps intended to give the Psalter a similarity in form to the five books of the Torah. This suggestion seems to be borne out by the placement at the beginning of the entire collection of Psalm 1, a psalm which sings the praises of the Torah. The divisions between these five books of the Psalter are marked by the insertion of short doxologies at the end of Psalms 41, 72, 89, and 106, and by the addition of Psalm 150 at the end. The basic tone which in Miriam's song marked the beginning of song in Israel also dominates the greatest collection of Israel's songs.

Some of the stages in the growth of the Psalter can be discerned. The doxology at the end of Psalm 72 (v. 19) is followed by this notice: "The prayers of David, the son of Jesse, are ended." The heading "of David" indicates that Psalms 3–41 and 51–72 belong to this collection. It is the view of modern scholarship that this designation is not so much an indication of the actual authorship of the Psalms as an expression of the high esteem in which David was held as the founder of Israel's worship in Jerusalem, as we find it expressed in the books of Chronicles (see above, p. 56). The heading designates the Psalms as suitable for use in the official cultic worship in Jerusalem. Smaller collections were ascribed to Korah (42–49) and Asaph (73–83), that is, to families of musicians in Jerusalem. Pilgrimage songs were collected in Psalms 120–134. In Psalms 42–83 the name Yahweh is replaced by "God" ("Elohim"), and therefore this collection is called the "Elohistic Psalter" (cf. Ps. 14 with Ps. 53). It is extremely difficult to date any of the individual psalms. For our understanding of the function of the psalms the analysis of their form and their relationship to the life of the community or of an individual is of more importance than finding the date when they were written (see above, p. 76).

The Form of the Hymns

The hymns have two essential elements in their form: the exhortation to praise and the reason for giving praise. "O give thanks to the Lord, for he is good" (Ps. 136:1). This corresponds to the ancient song of victory or deliverance (Exod. 15:21). As regards the exhortation, a group of people there present but not identified may be called on to praise Yahweh.

We should assume that there was a song leader. He could call on the whole assembly or on individual groups to sing: "Let Israel say, 'His steadfast love endures for ever.' Let the house of Aaron say, 'His steadfast love endures for ever' " (Ps. 118:2–4). In isolated cases, such as Psalm 150, the exhortation becomes the entire psalm. The most concise, often repeated form is "Hallelujah," that is, "Praise Yahweh." There were many possible variations. The hymn took on the form of a confession of faith when the group called on itself to give praise: "O come, let us sing to the Lord" (95:1). This element of confession becomes even clearer in the hymns of individuals: "I will give thanks to the Lord with my whole heart, in the company of the upright, in the congregation" (111:1). Finally, there is the form in which an individual calls on himself to give praise: "Bless the Lord, O my soul; and all that is within me, bless his holy name" (103:1). Here the individual becomes his own song leader.

The reasons given for offering praise also show a wealth of variation. Originally this element of the hymn probably expressed the praise of the assembled community, as seems to have been the case with the refrain in Psalm 136. In each verse, after the call to praise, God is presented and something is said about his deeds. In the second part of each verse, God is praised with the statement, "For his steadfast love endures for ever," probably sung by the congregation. The lives of those who are listening can be oriented in terms of the reasons given for praising God. What God has done for the world since creation, and what he has done for Israel since the slaying of the firstborn in Egypt, can move the people to praise him, because his faithfulness continues to be at work. The people praise God's deeds and attributes in declarative sentences or in participial phrases. Without praise, worship would have lost its purpose and its reason for existing. It is in the hymn that Israel came to self-knowledge.

Songs of Thanksgiving

Songs of thanksgiving are related to a specific experience of an individual. They are a part of the life of the community, but in them an individual is celebrating by a particular offering of thanks (Pss. 22:26 f.; 66:13–16; Jonah 2:10). In these songs the focus shifts. First the singer addresses the assembled group; he tells the reason why he is giving thanks, and always recounts specific factors: the danger in which he found himself, his call to God for help, and God's hearing his call. The threefold account is the clearest indicator of a song of thanks (Pss. 18:5–7; 22:25; 32:3–5; 118:5; Jonah 2:3–8). Often the singer draws a lesson from his experience. "It is better to take refuge in the Lord than to put confidence in man" (Ps. 118:8). "Many are the pangs of the wicked; but steadfast love surrounds him who trusts in the Lord" (32:10). This indicates an important qualification for becoming a teacher. Anyone who can report that Yahweh has heard his prayer in a time of trouble is qualified to tell Yahweh's name to his brethren (22:22).

The one giving thanks also turned to Yahweh and spoke a brief prayer of thanks, which was perhaps frequently repeated when sacrifice was offered, "I thank thee that thou hast answered me" (Ps. 118:21; Jonah 2:10; cf. Ps. 30:1). The entire congregation probably joined in with a hymn of praise (Pss. 118:1–4, 29; 32:11; cf. 22:27–31). Thus did the thanksgiving of individuals renew and extend the joy that people in Israel had in God.

Songs of Lament

The songs of lament are presupposed in the songs of thanksgiving, which regularly point back to them and even quote parts of them. An example is Jon. 2:4, "Then I said, 'I am cast out from thy presence; how shall I again look upon thy holy temple?' " Laments of the entire community as well as of individuals have been preserved. In part the community laments accept the troubles as the judgment which the prophets had foretold, but remembering that God had chosen them, the people ask if Yahweh is going to abandon them forever (Pss. 60:1–3; 74:1–3; 80:1–3). The elements of this category are the same as those of the individual laments, which are much more numerous in the Psalter.

The first word in many laments is "Yahweh" (Pss. 3:1; 6:1; 7:1; replaced in the Elohistic Psalter by "God," as in 54:1; 55:1; 56:1). In any case, God is invoked in the first sentence (5:1; 13:1; 17:1), often with the plea that he will hear (5:1; 17:1; 55:1). In Israel there was no uncertainty about whom to turn to in times of trouble. This assurance took its most concise form in the cry "My God" (13:1; 22:1; 88:1), but it could also be expressed and developed in declarations of confidence of varying length: "In thee our fathers trusted; they trusted, and thou didst deliver them. To thee they cried, and were saved; in thee they trusted and were not disappointed" (22:4–5). The individual finds support in the experience of all Israel: "But thou, O Lord, art enthroned for ever; thy name endures to all generations" (102:12). He can also base his confidence on the experiences of his own life: "Yet thou art he who took me from the womb. ... Upon thee was I cast from my birth" (22:9–10). He can commend himself succinctly to Yahweh as one who belongs to him and trusts in him (86:2). Often the description of the troubles comes first, as in 86:1, "I am poor and needy." The troubles are sometimes described at length: sickness (88:3–9*a*), persecution (140:1–5), false accusation (109:2–5). Sometimes the reasons for the lament are so expressed that each sufferer can include his own misery in such a formula, especially when the heart of the trouble is said to be abandonment by God (22:1–2, 6–8, 12–18). Distress is heard in the

typical rhetorical questions that express the despair of the one
praying: "Dost thou work wonders for the dead?" (88:10). The
words "why" (22:1; 74:1, 11; 88:14) and "how long" (13:1;
74:10; 79:5) are typical. As the person examines himself he
often confronts the question of guilt. A protestation of innocence can appeal to Yahweh's righteousness (5:4–7; 17:1–5),
and a confession of guilt can appeal to his mercy (86:2–3;
143:2). Often a vow is made, to be paid when the prayer is
heard (61:5); it may be a promise of offerings (56:12) or of
praise (71:22–24). All the prayers of lament find their point
in the petition that Yahweh hear those who pray (86:6; 88:2),
and return and be near to them again (22:11). Thus the formulas of lament offer to those who are crushed and despairing a
path of hope based on the experiences of Israel.

Three subcategories of lament require special attention. The
first is that of the so-called imprecatory psalms. These psalms
contain petitions that focus attention on the fate of the enemies
who have caused trouble for the one praying. They paint in
broad and specific terms the punishment that should fall on
these enemies. The desire for righteousness is aroused by the
sight of malice, spite, and a lust for vengeance (Pss. 69:22–28;
109:6–19; 137:7–9). Those who offer these prayers do not
intend to take revenge themselves; they are asking Yahweh to do
so. Instead of feeling superior to the authors of Israel's vengeful
psalms we of today should rather feel regret that with our
vengeful actions we still fall below the standard of ancient
Israel (cf. Rom. 12:19–21). In the presence of Israel's God,
even human rage may be permitted to express itself. If, however, wrath is truly left in God's hands, then it must sink into
silence before him, because Israel itself, with its own guilt, lives
by the mercy of God.

The psalms of confession are aware of this. The confesser laments his own failings as the greatest trouble encountered (see the quotation at 32:5 in a psalm of thanks). He laments that "no man living is righteous before" God (143:2), that all evil is a transgression against Yahweh and can be purged only by him, and that therefore the only possible sacrifice is a "broken and contrite heart" (51:5, 7–9, 16–17). If Israel hopes for life that can endure, it must wait for Yahweh's words of forgiveness, more than watchmen watch for the morning (130:3–4, 6–8).

The psalms of vengeance gave special expression to petition, and the psalms of confession stressed guilt. The psalms of confidence, however, give independent expression to that element of the form that led the one praying away from lamentation over trouble and toward hopeful petition. Psalm 16 begins with the final element of a lament, a petition, "Preserve me, O God, for in thee I take refuge," and then in what follows gives full expression to confidence in God. It is based on the ancient ordinance for the support of the Levites: "I am your portion and your inheritance among the people of Israel," Yahweh had told them (Num. 18:20; Deut. 10:9). The Levites did not live off their own property. "The Lord is my chosen portion and my cup; thou holdest my lot. The lines have fallen for me in pleasant places; yes, I have a goodly heritage" (Ps. 16:5–6). From this the one praying concludes that no threat, not even that of death, can separate him from Yahweh: "Therefore my heart is glad. ... Thou dost show me the path of life" (16:9–10). Psalm 23 is a pure psalm of confidence, with its pictorial language of Yahweh as shepherd and host, whose goodness follows the one praying more effectively than his enemies can; the house of the Lord is always open for him (23:6).

Songs of Zion

The songs of Zion show us that the sanctuary in Jerusalem was more than a place of refuge and security for individuals. Zion was first of all a guarantee for the whole community that "the Lord of hosts is with us; the God of Jacob is our refuge" (Ps. 46:7, 11). Because of Yahweh's choice of David and Mount Zion, there was additional reason to praise him (Ps. 132). As a result there developed a new way of praising the God of Zion (Pss. 46; 48; 76; 84; 87; 112). Scholars have observed here interesting features that had been retained from the pre-Israelite cult of the Jebusites. The habitation of the "Most High" is a bulwark against the raging nations (46:5–6). There was a time in which the person in danger could measure the greatness of his God by counting the towers of Jerusalem (48:12–13). The name of Jerusalem was seen as a sign of peace, because "Salem" was a reminder of "shalom," peace (122:6–8).

The Royal Psalms

The royal psalms document another way in which praise and lament were made concrete. It is astonishing that there are so few psalms—about ten—that specifically mention the king. He is the center of only one, the wedding song of Psalm 45. Other psalms are intercessions for him, because in Israel the name of Yahweh—not chariots and horses—is the source of confidence, even for the king (Ps. 20:7; cf. Ps. 21). They boast of the manifestation of Yahweh's faithfulness in the covenant with David (89:3–4), even in times of trouble (89:49–51). At every coronation these songs kept the great hope alive for the coming of the "son of God," who had a special relationship with the nations (Pss. 2; 110) and with the oppressed in the land (Ps. 72).

Hymns of Yahweh's Kingship

The hymns of Yahweh's kingship can be distinguished from the royal psalms, which are concerned with the Davidic king as a guarantee of Yahweh's help. They have the typical expression "Yahweh is king!" (Pss. 47:7; 93:1; 96:10; 97:1; 99:1). These hymns are the climax of the praise of Israel. There is no evidence that they were part of an enthronement festival of Yahweh along the lines of the festival in Babylon. Against such a possibility is the fact that Yahweh's throne is praised as having been "established from of old" (93:2). The one who established the world (93:1; 96:10) is superior to all current opponents (93:3–4). "The mountains melt like wax before the Lord" (97:5). The one who reigns in Zion (93:5; 99:2) is also "king of all the earth" (47:7). "All the gods of the peoples are idols" (96:5), and they must bow down before Yahweh (97:7). Thus the nations join together with the "people of the God of Abraham" in praising Yahweh (47:9; 96:7). In the praise of her savior, Israel becomes the song leader of the entire world. By the hymns of the choir the assurance that Yahweh is ruler of all the world is proclaimed to the ends of the earth. Praise has now become eschatological, because in the present it proclaims the expectation "He comes! He comes!" For what purpose? To establish his faithfulness and justice among all the peoples (96:13; 98:9). All nations and peoples should prepare to acclaim him (96:7–9; 98:4). Streams and forests will join in and clap their hands, and mountains and seas will roar (96:11–12; 98:7–8).

When we survey the categories of psalms we understand why the Psalter is called the book of praise. It is Israel's gift to the world. By looking to Yahweh, everything that has happened in the past and everything that is yet to come can move man in the present to praise. The absence of praise would signal the loss of biblical theology, or more specifically, that the God of Israel has been forgotten. When we remember him and what he has done, even our laments become expressions of confidence. The Psalter leads us to a new knowledge of the world, to the courage to hope, and to new worship of God, while the shadows of the false, crippling, illusory gods disappear.

Lamentations

The little book of Lamentations of Jeremiah provides an example of this. It is used in the synagogue on the day of mourning for the destruction of the Temple. It is a collection of five long laments which were written soon after the catastrophe that befell the city and the Temple, and were later ascribed to Jeremiah. In the middle of them, in chapter 3, the voice of an individual is heard. Inescapable troubles, unheard prayers, and confusing roads have shaken his trust in Yahweh (Lam. 3:1–18). Then he realizes that his dwelling on his trouble is itself a poison (v. 19). He comes to the point where he can state with confidence that Yahweh's faithfulness is great and new every morning (vv. 21–24). He comes to realize what wise men know, that it is good to wait quietly for Yahweh's help and to bear the yoke in one's youth (vv. 25–38). The one praying asks what right a person has to complain about anything, except his own shortcomings (v. 39). So he comes to the conclusion, "Let us test and examine our ways, and return to the Lord!" (v. 40). In meditating on his troubles he had shackled himself, but worship has now shown him his true situation and freed him for new expectations and changed conduct.

Because of the category to which it belongs, the book of Lamentations is discussed here alongside the Psalms. In the canon of the Hebrew Bible and of the Greek and Latin Bibles it is found at other places.

EXCURSUS: *The Order of Books in the Bible*

The order of books in the Bible requires special explanation. We must distinguish three forms of the canon, three different listings of the biblical books: the Hebrew canon (see above, p. 5), the Greek and Latin canon, and the canon agreed on at the Reformation. The last of these differs from the Hebrew canon only in the order of the books, whereas the Greek and Latin canon includes additional materials. The rearrangement of books involves the third part of the Hebrew canon, the "Writings," which since the Middle Ages have had the following order: Psalms, Job, Proverbs, the Five Scrolls or *Megilloth* (Ruth, Song of Solomon, Ecclesiastes, Lamentations, Esther), Daniel, Ezra, Nehemiah, and Chronicles. In the Greek and Latin canon and in the Reformation canon, five books of this third section, because of their nature as poetical or instructional books, were placed between the historical books (Torah and the Former Prophets) and the prophetic books (Later Prophets). They were given the following order: Job, Psalms, Proverbs, Ecclesiastes, and Song of Solomon. The rest of the "Writings" were assigned on the basis of content to one or the other of the three new divisions: history, instruction, and prophecy. Because of its historical content, Ruth was placed after the Book of Judges, and for the same reason Chronicles, Ezra, Nehemiah, and Esther, in this new order, were placed after the books of Kings. The Lamentations were thought to have been written by Jeremiah, and so they were placed after the Book of Jeremiah. Daniel was included among the major prophets, after Ezekiel.

The Latin Bible differs from this Reformation canon by the inclusion of the apocryphal books of Tobit and Judith after Esther; Wisdom and Sirach after the Song of Solomon; Baruch after Lamentations; and Maccabees after Malachi. The Greek Bible has additional supplements, as well as a different order for the following books: Job comes between Song of Solomon and Wisdom; the Minor Prophets before Isaiah; and Hosea-Amos-Micah before Joel-Obadiah-Jonah. A knowledge of these different forms of the canon makes it easier to find your way around in different editions of the Bible.

WISDOM AND INSTRUCTION: PSALMS, PROVERBS AND DIDACTIC STORIES

In Israel, wisdom literature took various forms. These range from the brief proverb through the didactic poem and didactic story to a fully developed dialogue.

Didactic Poetry in the Psalter

The Psalter contains several didactic poems. The very first psalm displays the characteristics of wisdom literature: the wish for the special relationship called "blessed"; the contrast of opposing activities ("not in the counsel of the wicked . . . but his delight is in the law of the Lord"), and their results ("the wicked will not stand in the judgment . . . the Lord knows the way of the righteous"); and the use of metaphors from the world of nature ("yields its fruit"; "chaff which the wind drives away"). The content of Psalm 1 invites the reader to share the joy of the Torah and of its constant study (v. 2). Other Torah psalms are 19:8–15 and 119. Both of them, like Psalm 1, deal with the individual. Psalm 119 begins with praise. It provides a convenient aid to memorization in that the twenty-two letters of the Hebrew alphabet are used in sequence to begin each group of 8 verses—an alphabetic acrostic. All 176 verses contain at least one of eight terms which Israel used to designate Yahweh's revelation: law, testimonies, precepts, statutes, commandments, ordinances, word, and way. Most verses are in the form of a prayer. The basic mood is one of joy: "And I shall walk at liberty, for I have sought thy precepts" (v. 45). The consequences of actions are considered: "When I think of thy ways, I turn my feet to thy testimonies" (v. 59). God's word dethrones the natural authorities: "I understand more than the aged, for I keep thy precepts" (v. 100). This is the way people were made acquainted with Scripture.

Other didactic psalms have as their theme the fear of Yahweh, that is, obedience. Psalm 34 is also in the form of an alphabetic acrostic. As in the songs of thanks (see above, p. 106) the basis for instruction is the fact that prayer has been answered: "This poor man cried, and the Lord heard him. . . . O taste and see that the Lord is good!" (34:6, 8). Then follow various forms of instruction, such as exhortations, questions, categorical advice, and proverbs (vv. 9–21). The wisdom psalms 112, 128, and 133 praise particularly the happy consequences of fearing Yahweh. Psalm 127 declares that fortune and misfortune are decided by our attitude to Yahweh, and Psalm 139 helps us search our consciences.

The great history psalm, Psalm 78, is also to be regarded as didactic. A general didactic introduction calls the hearer to pay attention to the traditions of the ancestors. This instruction brings past and future generations together (vv. 1–4), because in Israel hope for the future and remembrance of past history are inseparable. This is why the hearers are to pass the teaching on to their descendants, "so that they should set their hope in God, and not forget the works of God, but keep his commandments" (v. 7). Next, the history from the time of the exodus down to the choice of Zion and David is recounted (vv. 12–72), including both Yahweh's deeds and the generally disobedient reactions of the people.

Psalms 37, 49, and 73 wrestle with the difficult question about God's righteousness, given the suffering of the innocent.

They know that unrighteousness is not always followed by disaster, and fear of God is not always followed by blessing. He alone is wise who can wait for the end (73:17), remain true to Yahweh even when body and soul waste away, and find his joy in the presence of Yahweh (73:23–28). True wisdom knows the limits of its searching and knowing.

Proverbs

The book of Proverbs is a comprehensive collection of Israelite proverbial wisdom of the earlier times. Of later literature, only the book of Jesus Sirach (Ecclesiasticus) and the book of Wisdom can be compared to it.

The book as it now exists is composed of several older collections. When it received its final editing, the entire book was ascribed to "Solomon, son of David, king of Israel" (Prov. 1:1). This ascription contains a kernel of historical truth, because after the highly developed exhortations in chapters 1–9, the first collection of individual proverbs contains at 10:1 the brief heading "The proverbs of Solomon." Even if the crediting of the collection as such to the wise king is secondary, there is no reason to doubt that Solomon produced a great quantity of wisdom poetry (according to 1 Kings 4:32, three thousand proverbs and a thousand and five songs) and that his wisdom achieved international fame (1 Kings 4:31, 34; 10:1 ff.). His wisdom was compared with that of Egypt and that of the "people of the east" (1 Kings 4:30), among whom the Edomites were best known to Israel (Jer. 49:7; Obad. 8). After Solomon's time, wisdom was carefully cultivated in Israel. The next heading, "the words of the wise" (Prov. 22:17), is evidence for the existence of a teaching profession. In Jer. 18:18 "the wise" are mentioned along with priests and prophets. The proverbs contained in 22:17–23:11 are similar to the teachings of the Egyptian scribe Amenemope. Where did the teachers of wisdom have their school? The next heading, in 25:1, gives us the answer: "These also are proverbs of Solomon which the men of Hezekiah king of Judah copied." The Solomonic tradition must therefore have been perpetuated at the royal court in Jerusalem. In 30:1 ff. "The words of Agur" are added, and in 31:1 ff., "The words of Lemuel"—both collections being apparently of north Arabian or Edomite origin. Thus in this book of Proverbs the wisdom of Egypt and that of the people of the east were preserved together with the wisdom of Solomon and later teachers of Israel.

What forms of wisdom instruction do we find in the proverbs? The most common is the declaration (*mashal*). As a folk proverb it has a very simple form, for example, "Like mother, like daughter" (Ezek. 16:44). There is one rhyming proverb in this form: *ba zadon wayyabo kalon*, "When pride comes, then comes disgrace" (Prov. 11:2). The developed form added an antithesis to it, "but with the humble is wisdom." Proverbs of this type encapsule experience: "A gracious woman gets honor, and violent men get riches" (11:16). More artistic than these antitheses are such comparisons as "Like a dog that returns to his vomit is a fool that repeats his folly" (26:11). Especially popular were the forms with "better": "It is better to live in the corner of a housetop than in a house shared with a contentious woman" (25:24). It is only a short step from these statements which express in the indicative how things are to the advice which states in the imperative how things should be: "Let your foot be seldom in your neighbor's house, lest he become weary of you and hate you" (25:17). Exhortations of this type of proverb always point to the consequences of specific actions; they are not to be obeyed blindly, but tested. As a consequence, sometimes the description of the results of specific behavior takes up much more space than the advice itself: "Do not look at wine when it is red, when it sparkles in the cup and goes down smoothly. At the last it bites like a serpent, and stings like an adder. Your eyes will see strange things, and your mind utter perverse things. You will be like one who lies down in the midst of the sea, like one who lies on the top of a mast. 'They struck me,' you will say, 'but I was not hurt; they beat me, but I did not feel it. When shall I awake? I will seek another drink' " (23:31–35). The drinker is shown the consequences of his actions: blindness, confusion, staggering, unconsciousness, addiction. Education here takes the form of training in a rational view of how events are connected with each other. The last example cited has already crossed the border separating the proverb from the didactic poem. A riddle or a question too can be expanded into a larger form: "Who has woe? Who has sorrow? Who has strife? Who has complaining? Who has wounds without cause? Who has redness of eyes? Those who tarry long over wine, those who go to try mixed wine" (23:29–30). Riddles were probably also the source of the numerical proverb, in which a number of similar phenomena are brought together, for example, small creatures that are wise. "Four things on earth are small, but they are exceedingly wise: the ants are a people not strong, yet they provide their food in the summer; the badgers are a people not mighty, yet they make their homes in the rocks; the locusts have no king, yet all of them march in rank; the lizard you can take in your hands, yet it is in kings' palaces" (30:24–28; cf. 30:18–20). In chapters 1–9 we find extended forms—didactic poems and exhortations.

Themes of the Wisdom Literature

The themes of the wisdom literature are wide-ranging. Solomon, as the model teacher of wisdom, was praised for having as an essential attribute "largeness of mind like the sand on the seashore" (1 Kings 4:29). Four thematic areas are particularly prominent.

First, wisdom drawn from nature characterizes the numerical proverb cited above. It is reported that Solomon himself knew botany and zoology: "He spoke of trees, from the cedar that is in Lebanon to the hyssop that grows out of the wall; he spoke also of beasts, and of birds, and of reptiles, and of fish" (1 Kings 4:33).

We find an example from the area of legal judgment in the "Solomonic" decision rendered in the quarrel of two women over a child (1 Kings 3:16–28). Similar proverbs were probably used in the training of princes and government officials. "By justice a king gives stability to the land, but one who exacts gifts ruins it" (Prov. 29:4).

The largest amount of space is devoted to the area of educational wisdom, which could train a person how to behave in all aspects of his life, from his daily care for his own body, eating and drinking, the handling of money, relations with friends and with women, to the difficult art of knowing when to speak and when to keep silent. A few examples here may whet the appetite for reading further in the Proverbs. "As a door turns on its hinges, so does a sluggard on his bed" (26:14). "Pressing milk produces curds, pressing the nose produces blood, and pressing anger produces strife" (30:33)—in terms of the consequences, the way one treats his own nose is compared, in true wisdom fashion, with actions in nature and in human relations. Test your friends: "There are friends who pretend to be friends, but there is a friend who sticks closer than a brother" (18:24). Test women: "This is the way of an adulteress; she eats, and wipes her mouth, and says, 'I have done no wrong'" (30:20). Eat moderately: "Put a knife to your throat if you are a man given to appetite" (23:2). Good breeding demands that we know how to speak and how to keep silent: "A word fitly spoken is like apples of gold in a setting of silver" (25:11). "Like clouds and wind without rain is a man who boasts of a gift he does not give" (25:14). "He who sings songs to a heavy heart is like one who takes off a garment on a cold day, and like vinegar on a wound" (25:20).

Finally, the basis and limits of a wise life were explored in the area of theological wisdom. "The fear of the Lord is the beginning of knowledge" (Prov. 1:7). Yahweh is silently at work in the operation of the world, and this encourages people to seek things out. "It is the glory of God to conceal things, but the glory of kings is to search things out" (25:2). A wise man humbly considers what is possible: "A man's mind plans his way, but the Lord directs his steps" (16:9). Fear of Yahweh keeps a person from going astray in both small and great undertakings. "The Lord does not let the righteous go hungry, but he thwarts the craving of the wicked" (10:3). Research in the theology of the wisdom literature, which is so restrained in expression but for that very reason of fundamental importance, is one of the most important tasks of contemporary Old Testament scholarship.

Edifying Stories

The desire to impart instruction found a new form in several edifying stories. The short story of Jonah is particularly well written. It deals in a straightforward manner with questions that were agitating the postexilic community. What attitude should be taken toward Yahweh's unfulfilled threats against Israel's enemies? What position should Israel take in regard to its archenemies? What are the limits of Yahweh's mercy? A clear intention to teach is indicated by the very formulation of the questions with which the sailors assault Jonah: "What is your occupation? And whence do you come? . . . What is this that you have done?" (Jon. 1:8, 10). The questions which Yahweh asks are very pointed: "Do you do well to be angry?" (4:4, 9). And at the end the reader is left with a question directed to Jonah, "And should not I pity Nineveh?" (4:11). The teaching methods are surprising—a gradually intensifying repetition, and a striking stereotyping of the characters. We may compare the active, pious fear shown by the sailors (1:4, 10, 16) with the callous attitude of Jonah (1:9), and Jonah's grief over the plant with Yahweh's grief over Nineveh (4:8–11). The miracles of the fish and the plant are drawn into the teaching purpose of the book with a large dose of comedy and humor. Amid the consideration of serious and difficult problems, a restrained laughter becomes our teacher. The content of the book shows how Jonah, in fleeing from his task, encounters still other groups of foreigners (chap. 1), and how Jonah's petty self-pity reveals the falseness of his anger over Yahweh's compassion (chap. 4). The entire story serves to give a totally new interpretation to the traditional confession that Yahweh is a "gracious God and merciful, slow to anger, and abounding in steadfast love, and repentest of evil" (4:2; cf. Exod. 34:6; Joel 2:13). Jonah-Israel knows this very well, but Jonah-Israel is unwilling for God's grace to include the cruel world. How much stimulus there is here for new forms of teaching. It whets our appetite for more teaching of this sort.

Equally artistic is the little book of Ruth, although its teaching purpose is more restrained. In an idyllic secular setting, the faithfulness of a young Moabite woman is portrayed. Ruth had married the son of an Ephrathite family from Bethlehem that had come to live in her country. After becoming a widow, Ruth accompanies her mother-in-law, also a widow, back to Bethlehem. She movingly declares, "Where you go, I will go, and where you lodge I will lodge" (Ruth 1:16). At the time of the barley harvest—it was for this reason that the book became a part of the celebration of Pentecost, the festival of the grain harvest—Ruth becomes acquainted with Boaz, a relative of her father-in-law, and according to the law of levirate marriage (Deut. 25:5 ff.) he marries her, after going through the proper rites. She gives birth to a son named Obed, who at the end of the book is presented as the father of Jesse, and hence the ancestor of David (Ruth 4:17, 22). This drives home the point of this masterful story. It was directed against a haughty Jewish community that had shut itself off from the heathen nations around it and so had failed to know them as they really were. At the beginning of the Gospel of Matthew (1:5) there is a genealogy which identifies David's grandmother as a Moabite. Unobtrusively a broad-minded love is taught. Ruth is faithful to a poor and lonely Israelite woman, accepts her God (Ruth 1:16), cares for her, and then finds the love and protecting care of an Israelite man. The short stories of Jonah and Ruth showed to the late postexilic community that foreigners could be examples to imitate. Wisdom literature had taught the people of Israel anew that they could understand themselves correctly only in conjunction with the other nations.

The Book of Esther, written in Hellenistic times, is almost a historical novel. It is also one of the books read at the holy days, because it marks the founding of the festival of Purim, a popular festival celebrated on the fourteenth and fifteenth of Adar (February/March). With mounting suspense it depicts the planning of a persecution of the Jews in the Persian Empire. Queen Esther, herself a Jew, is urged by her guardian Mordecai to try to stop the measures which Haman, the enemy of the Jews, is taking with King Ahasuerus (Xerxes I). He tells her, "If you keep silence at such a time as this, relief and deliverance will rise for the Jews from another quarter" (Esther 4:14). Esther is ready to go to the king, even though it is "against the law." "If I perish, I perish," she says (4:16). And so finally the day set for the pogrom becomes a day on which the persecutors of the Jews perish gruesomely. Sorrow is turned into joy, and a new festival comes into being, days of "feasting and gladness, days for sending choice portions to one another and gifts to the poor" (9:22). The festival was called "Purim"—a term derived from the Babylonian word "Pur," meaning "lot"—because the casting of lots before Haman was the occasion for the events that followed (3:7; 9:24 ff.). The book celebrates Jewish cleverness and courage and can be seen as a secular counterpart to the Exodus tradition.

The Song of Solomon

An equally secular book is the Song of Solomon, which in Hebrew has the name "Song of Songs," meaning the most beautiful of songs. It was included among the festival scrolls because it had become a part of the celebration of the eighth day of Passover. This usage presupposes an allegorical interpretation of its contents in terms of the love of God for his people—a clearly secondary interpretation. The collection is actually made up of some thirty songs of purely human love, as is shown by its similarity to ancient Egyptian love songs. Numerous individual statements can be understood only in a secular sense. "Refresh me with apples, for I am sick with love" (Song of Sol. 2:5). "As a lily among brambles, so is my love among maidens" (2:2). The forms of comparison so familiar from the wisdom literature are used in the various categories of descriptive songs, admiration songs, and songs of longing. One of the few songs describing the girl's lover says: "His head is the finest gold; his locks are wavy, black as a raven. . . . His lips are lilies. . . . His body is ivory work. . . . This is my beloved" (5:11–16). Whether this style of poetry originated in part among the upper classes during the monarchy (Solomon appears here as patron in 1:1; 3:7, 9; 8:11), or whether it is the style of the postexilic wisdom poetry, it reflects the freedom with which the sexes associated with each other and a joy in the physical. "The voice of my beloved! Behold, he comes, leaping upon the mountains, bounding over the hills. My beloved is like a gazelle, or a young stag. Behold, there he stands behind our wall, gazing in at the windows, looking through the lattice. My beloved speaks and says to me: 'Arise, my love, my fair one, and come away' " (2:8–10). This eroticism is not regarded as demonic, nor is it deified; it is a great human achievement. The question of having children disappears entirely behind this mutual love, which Yahweh has aroused: "Its flashes are flashes of fire, a most vehement flame" (literally, "a flame of Yahweh"; 8:6).

This literature at the fringes of the canon shows how the arts of narrative and poetry include the ultimate passions—the grief of Yahweh himself over Nineveh's troubles in the Book of Jonah; the dedication of the little Moabite woman Ruth, who became the greatest mother and ancestress in Israel; the triumphant bravery of those who were persecuted in the Book of Esther; and the marvel of a love, which, far removed from marriage, flourished in secret intimacy ("I adjure you, O daughters of Jerusalem, by the gazelles or the hinds of the field, that you stir not up nor awaken love until it please" [Song of Sol. 3:5]), and that still can be fulfilled only in marriage ("I held him, and would not let him go until I had brought him into my mother's house, and into the chamber of her that conceived me" [3:4]). Thus even in this fringe literature we are once again exposed to the fullness of life in the Old Testament, from the heights of world history to the most secret intimacies.

EXCURSUS: *The Scholarly Literature of the Old Testament*

As we might expect, the scholarly study of the Old Testament, in keeping with the wisdom and instruction of the Old

Testament itself, ranges over extensive and diverse areas. For this reason it needs to make use of all the available help from other scholarly disciplines as it dedicates itself to its own main task, the exposition of the many and varied biblical texts. Old Testament studies in turn, as they set forth the distinctive teachings of the Old Testament, will mean a great deal for all of theology, especially for the theology of the New Testament and for systematic and practical theology.

Scholarly editions of the text are the starting point of all research. The Leningrad manuscript, as the oldest complete text available (see above, pp.73 f.), has been the basis of the *Biblia Hebraica* (edited by Rudolph Kittel) since the third edition (Stuttgart: Würtembergische Bibelanstalt, 1937), and of the *Biblia Hebraica Stuttgartensia,* which will replace it. This new critical edition of the Hebrew text was made necessary by the results of the study of the texts found near the Dead Sea. Critical editions of the ancient translations, Hebrew lexicons, such as that of Köhler-Baumgartner and the more concise one of Holladay, and grammars that deal adequately with Hebrew syntax enable a student to deal directly with the text.

Commentaries are designed to evaluate the results of special research and to present new tasks and new insights. The Old Testament Library (Philadelphia: Westminster, 1961–) gives clear and lucid explanations of the text and its background. The Anchor Bible (Garden City, N.Y.: Doubleday, 1964–) gives more detailed philological material. Hermeneia (Philadelphia: Fortress, 1971–) is projected as a thorough critical and historical commentary. In addition, many older works are available in English, as well as several series of more limited scope.

Much specific research appears first in articles in journals, two of which are devoted exclusively to the Old Testament. The *Zeitschrift für die alttestamentliche Wissenschaft* (published since 1881) contains book reviews and reports on articles in other journals in addition to its own articles. *Vetus Testamentum* has been published since 1951 in Leiden, in the Netherlands. The *Journal of Biblical Literature* contains technical articles on the entire Bible, and *Interpretation* deals more with the interpretation and the theology of biblical texts. There are also commentaries and general works on the Old Testament that are published individually.

A number of comprehensive works present the results of the scholarly labors of the last several generations. Among the most useful are John Bright's *A History of Israel* (2d ed.; Philadelphia: Westminster, 1972); Martin Noth's *The Old Testament World* (Philadelphia: Fortress, 1966); Artur Weiser's *The Old Testament: Its Formation and Development* (New York: Association Press, 1961); *The Old Testament and Modern Study*, edited by H. H. Rowley (New York: Oxford University, 1951); Roland de Vaux's *Ancient Israel* (New York: McGraw-Hill, 1961); Helmer Ringgren's *Israelite Religion* (Philadelphia: Fortress, 1966); and Gerhard von Rad's *Old Testament Theology* (New York: Harper & Row, 1962).

RIDDLES AND PERPLEXITIES: ECCLESIASTES, JOB AND DANIEL

In every age Israel was confronted with problems, some more troublesome than others. Israel's experiences with Yahweh usually revealed the greater depths of the problems and prevented easy solutions. In some of the later books of the Old Testament, all of life becomes one big riddle, and the nature of God himself is hidden by clouds.

Ecclesiastes

The book of Ecclesiastes is more accessible to the nihilists at the close of the second Christian millennium than any other book of the Bible. Sartre, Camus, and many others bear witness to this. Its language and themes can best be understood against the background of the third century B.C., when, under the Ptolemies, both Jews and Greeks were raising the same questions. Luther called the book "The Preacher," following the name it bears in the Greek Bible. The Greek Ecclesiastes was a translation of the Hebrew *Qoheleth*, which could be rendered more accurately as "leader of an assembly." The word may also be a pseudonym for the author, who conceals his identity behind that of a descendant of David, a king in Jerusalem (Eccles. 1:1, 12). What he says shows him to be a very late participant in that wisdom movement which had taken Solomon as its authority, but he himself lived and worked on the fringes of that tradition.

As one of the scrolls used at the great festivals, Ecclesiastes belongs to the Feast of Tabernacles (Succoth), in which the memories of the journey through the wilderness are preserved. This usage perhaps indicates a realization that the book is a part of that everyday life in which men and women must confront the burdens of life without prophets or miracles to help them, and even without that wisdom which was the "hostess" to earlier generations (Prov. 9:1). The customary wisdom forms of statements and exhortations are missing. They are replaced by a broader form of reflections in which observations and experiences are opposed to assured conclusions. The reader will discover two or more profound negative insights set in immediate juxtaposition, paradoxically enough, to one easily grasped bit of positive advice.

Empty abysses surround the book. Its first sentence sounds the theme: "Vanity of vanities, says the Preacher, vanity of vanities! All is vanity" (Eccles. 1:2). And as the conclusion of all his reflections he repeats, "Vanity of vanities, says the Preacher; all is vanity" (12:8). The New English Bible translates the term as "emptiness." The Hebrew word designated the blowing wind, as a symbol of the unstable and impermanent. How did the "Preacher" come to this truly devastating judgment on everything in life? In earlier times the wisdom movement was directed toward the fullness of life. "And I applied my mind to seek and to search out by wisdom all that is done under heaven; it is an unhappy business that God has given to the sons of men to be busy with" (1:13). How did it happen that the joy in seeking and searching turned into boredom? "Man cannot find out the work that is done under the sun. However much man may toil in seeking, he will not find it out; even though a wise man claims to know, he cannot find it out" (8:17). What causes the failure of human knowledge? Wisdom's basic thesis about the connection between deeds and their rewards does not hold water: "The wise man has his eyes in his head, but the fool walks in darkness; and yet I perceived that one fate comes to all of them" (2:14). "In my vain life I have seen everything; there is a righteous man who perishes in his righteousness, and there is a wicked man who prolongs his life in his evil-doing. Be not righteous overmuch, and do not make yourself overwise; why should you destroy yourself?" (7:15–16). Here the nihilistic irony breaks through! "He does not know what is to be, for who can tell him how it will be?" (8:7). "For who knows what is good for man while he lives the few days of his vain life, which he passes like a shadow?" (6:12). Because an individual can see neither the connections among things nor the future, Qoheleth came to say, "So I turned about and gave my heart up to despair" (2:20a), so that he envied the dead, and, even more, those who had never been born (4:2 f.). This is the deepest melancholy found anywhere in the canon. Life itself has made all wisdom useless, because the individual cannot grasp the whole of life.

But there is more to be said. God himself has made this wisdom useless. It should be noted that "Yahweh," the name of Israel's God, is never used in this book. In contrast to Esther, however, God is spoken of and is even one of the themes of the book. All the trouble that roots in a lack of knowledge of the world would disappear if the knowledge of God were not lacking. "As you do not know how the spirit comes to the bones in the womb of a woman with child, so you do not know the work of God who makes everything" (11:5). Qoheleth remains convinced that he "saw all the work of God, that man cannot find out the work that is done under the sun" (8:17). Man sees only fragments: "For everything there is a season . . . a time to be born, and a time to die; . . . a time to mourn, and a time to dance; . . . a time to embrace, and a time to refrain from embracing. . . . He has made everything beautiful in its time; also he has put eternity into man's mind, yet so that he cannot find out what God has done from the beginning to the end" (3:1–11). And so men and women are not to talk about God too much: "God is in heaven, and you upon earth; therefore let your words be few" (5:2). In great sincerity the writer here documents the fact that it is impossible to gain a knowledge of God out of the total phenomena of the world.

What are we to do, then, in the light of the fact that life is useless and we cannot know God in the world? It is remarkable that the preacher does not end up either by giving up his life or by falling into sensuality. This is explained by another remarkable feature of the book. It is precisely where the question of proper behavior crops up that the writer speaks of God, his acts and his gifts to men; this is a remnant of typical Israelite belief. After it has been established that we cannot know all that God is doing, we read, "I know that there is nothing better for them than to be happy and enjoy themselves as long as they live; also that it is God's gift to man that everyone should eat and drink and take pleasure in all his toil" (Eccles. 3:12–13), "the few days of his life which God has given him" (5:18). "Enjoy life with the wife whom you love, all the days of your vain life which he has given you under the sun" (9:9). Work is a part of it: "Whatever your hand finds to do, do it with your might" (9:10). Be serious: "Remember also your Creator in the days of your youth, before the evil days come . . . when the keepers of the house tremble, and the strong men are bent" (12:1–3). Don't overdo your efforts: "My son, beware of anything beyond these. Of making many books there is no end, and much study is a weariness of the flesh" (12:12). The epilogue reminds us that fear of God is the standard for judgment (12:13 f.), for it opens our eyes to the trees in the midst of the forest. The slightest remembrance of Israel's knowledge of the Creator keeps this almost nihilistic skeptic on the narrow line between despair and arrogance: "Consider the work of God; who can make straight what he has made crooked? In the day of prosperity be joyful, and in the day of adversity consider; God has made the one as well as the other, so that man may not find out anything that will be after him" (7:13–14). Men and women of today who can no longer understand the world and God will find a neighbor in the "Preacher," a neighbor who, in the midst of the uselessness of life, will open their eyes for the pleasures that are still there for them to enjoy.

Job

The Book of Job not only takes its readers along the path of resignation but also catches them up in rebellion against the God of the theologians. The first thing to notice in Job are the different literary strands with their diverse statements of the problem. The framework of the book consists of an edifying folktale that reflects an Edomite background. By alternating scenes in heaven with scenes on earth it gains the reader's interest and holds him in suspense (Job 1–2; 41:7–17). Within this framework a highly artistic dialogue unfolds between Job and his three friends, Eliphaz, Bildad, and Zophar. After Job's introductory lament in chapter 3, each of the three friends is to speak in each of three cycles of speeches, and Job answers each of their speeches (chaps. 4–14; 15–21; 22–27; in the third cycle Zophar's speech is missing). In a great concluding speech Job makes a final appeal to the hidden, silent God. And in 38:1–42:6 there follows, finally, God's answer as he speaks—twice—out of the whirlwind (38:1 ff.; 40:6 ff.), each of the two sections being followed by Job's words of submission (40:1 ff.; 42:1 ff.). The literary historian faces several problems here, because there have obviously been additions. Nevertheless, the total outline and the connection between the dialogue of the friends and the speeches of God and Job's remorse remain uncontested as a poetic work. Only two major passages are to be distinguished from this context. The first is the great poem in praise of wisdom in chapter 28, which portrays wisdom, in contrast to human presumption, as totally beyond man's capacity to discover it: "God understands the way to it, and he knows its place" (28:23). The second is the speeches of Elihu in chapters 32–37, whose basic theme is that suffering is designed to purify the sufferer. Both additions deserve close attention, but here we must limit ourselves simply to the overall framework and to the great poetic dialogue.

The prose framework holds the reader in suspense by means of a dramatic alternation between scenes on earth and scenes in heaven. Its main focus is on the conditions of Job's piety, that is to say, his total loyalty to Yahweh. The first scene on earth shows a rich Job maintaining his relationship with God in the face of sins his children may have committed, but in the following scene in the heavenly court, Satan, as the heavenly prosecutor, raises the question of whether Job fears God "for naught." Yahweh agrees to Satan's suggestion of testing his "servant" Job by taking away all Job's possessions. Satan is here the accuser and the representative of the opposition, but still clearly subordinate to Yahweh. Along with all the heavenly beings, the reader watches appalled as the devastating events of the third scene unfold. One after another messengers arrive bringing the news that all Job's possessions, his servants, and his children have perished. But Job, ignorant of the heavenly decision to test him, prays, "The Lord gave, and the Lord has taken away; blessed be the name of the Lord" (1:21). The second heavenly council leads to an even more extreme test; loathsome disease attacks Job himself. Temptation assumes the voice of the only surviving member of his family—his wife. She says, "Do you still hold fast your integrity? Curse God, and die" (2:9). Job rejects this advice as stupid: "Shall we receive good at the hand of God, and shall we not receive evil?" (2:10). So the opponent in heaven is defeated by this suffering servant of Yahweh, who at the end is vindicated and given a new fullness of life. Here we find taught a fear of God that can confront the riddle of God's hidden decisions, and, even in deepest suffering, remain faithful to God. The conviction that Yahweh is sovereign leads to complete submission.

In the dialogue, on the other hand, Job resists vigorously, and the question of the righteousness of God is stated sharply by all the means at the poet's command. Form critics are uncertain whether the speeches that are exchanged are to be interpreted as didactic arguments, as legal processes, or in terms of sacral law. The lament in chapter 3 plunges us into the initial situation where there is no comfort possible for Job, and he calls down curses on the day of his birth. For no reason at all God had closed every road open before him (3:23). The teachings of the "friends" attempt to answer this despairing attitude along a broad front. Attempts have been made to distinguish the characters of the three, but it is more productive to look at the forms their speeches take and the arguments they advance. In maxims, bits of advice, reflections, and parables the fullness of traditional wisdom literature is brought forward (8:8 ff.). Eliphaz even brings up a prophetic vision which he had seen (4:12–21). Job was confronted by both theology and pastoral concern, expressed sometimes in a desire to be helpful, sometimes impudently, but always self-confidently. Basically the dispute centers around the great international teachings of wisdom concerning the connection between deeds and destiny: "Think now, who that was innocent ever perished? Or where were the upright cut off?" (4:7). Job's suffering must be the consequence of some serious, hidden guilt. In one attempt after another Job is urged to recognize this guilt, forsake it, and submit himself to God. In this, these theologians do not even come up to the standards of the teaching in the larger framework.

Job already knows all the bits of wisdom that they hold up before him. "No doubt you are the people, and wisdom will die with you" (12:2). With scorn, with questions, with shouts of terror, and with his unrelenting demand for justice, Job holds out against the attempts of his friends to reduce his suffering and God's justice to a common denominator of traditional wisdom. "It is all one; therefore I say, he destroys both the blameless and the wicked" (9:22; cf. 27:5). "If I wash myself with snow, and cleanse my hands with lye, yet thou wilt plunge me into a pit" (9:30 f.). Job sees himself as the victim of an arbitrary use of power. "How long wilt thou not look away from me, nor let me alone till I swallow my spittle? If I sin, what do I do to thee, thou watcher of men? Why hast thou made me thy mark?" (7:19–20).

Thus Job challenges God more and more to defend himself;

the friends cannot give him any answer: "There is no umpire between us who might lay his hand upon us both" (9:33). In his rebellion against God, it is only to God himself that Job can turn: "Even now, behold, my witness is in heaven, and he that vouches for me is on high" (16:19). Even if he is completely swallowed up by death, Job still says, "I know that my Redeemer lives, and at last he will stand upon the earth" (19:25). And in a final solemn oath protesting his innocence he exclaims, "Oh, that I had one to hear me! (Here is my signature! let the Almighty answer me!)" (31:35). Then follow the words of God out of the whirlwind (chaps. 38–41). Question after question is hurled at Job. "Who is this that darkens counsel by words without knowledge? . . . Where were you when I laid the foundation of the earth?" (38:2, 4). And then God lets his creation speak for him. In the testimony that God bears to himself Job's complaints are silenced: "I had heard of thee by the hearing of the ear, but now my eye sees thee" (42:5). God himself has won back the one who rebelled against him. Only God could do it.

Daniel

The Book of Daniel, in the "Writings," is the youngest part of the Old Testament canon. A survey of its contents shows that we must distinguish several strands which indicate different points of origin. The reader is immediately aware of the differences in form and content between the two halves of the book. The first six chapters contain stories about Daniel, but chapters 7–12 contain four visions in which Daniel speaks in the first person.

The stories place Daniel in the time of the early captivity in Babylon under Nebuchadnezzar (Dan. 1:1–2). For Ezekiel, Daniel was, along with Noah and Job, an exemplary righteous man in the dim past, about whom there was nothing more to say

(Ezek. 14:14, 20). The stories of our book, on the other hand, picture him as a wise, highly cultured man, who maintains loyalty to a foreign state but also enters into sharp conflicts that prove his loyalty to the faith. The narrator is obviously presenting legends intended to remind his contemporaries, who are living in similar circumstances, of how the past can serve as an example of wise behavior in relation to the heathen state and also of unbroken trust in God's faithfulness and sovereign power. That the author was far removed from the time of the exile is shown by his completely false portrayals of the Babylonian, Median, and Persian rulers. With respect to the date of the book, it is important to note that the stories in chapters 2–6, and also chapter 7, are written in the Aramaic language. Scholars have still not solved the riddle of why the transition from Hebrew to Aramaic and back again does not correspond with the division of the book between stories and visions. Perhaps the stories are older than the visions, because the visions show much more tension in the relationship to the political powers than do the legends of the men in the fiery furnace in chapter 3, and of Daniel in the lions' den. Both of these stories end with the foreign king giving particular honor to those who had been persecuted. Daniel, the wise interpreter of dreams, is a member of the king's innermost circle of advisers in chapters 2, 4, and 5.

The visions bring us unmistakably to the days of Antiochus IV Epiphanes, specifically to those years when this Seleucid king had forbidden the faithful in Jerusalem to observe their worship ceremonies and had desecrated the Temple. He is the one who is meant in Dan. 7:25, "He shall speak words against the Most High, and shall think to change the times and the law." In 12:11 we read about "the time that the continual burnt offering is taken away, and the abomination that makes desolate is set up" (cf. 8:13 f.; 9:27; 11:36 f.). Each of the four visions in chapters 7, 8, 9, and 10–12 fits therefore precisely in this period. The attacks of Antiochus IV on the Jerusalem cult took place in the year 167 B.C. The visions do not reveal any knowledge of the success of the Maccabean uprising and the rededication of the Temple by Judas Maccabaeus in 164 B.C. They may, however, date from the period when the success of the Maccabees nourished hopes of a new turn in events. The seer speaks repeatedly of a period of about three and a half years during which the arrogant ruler holds sway, as, for instance, in 7:25*b*, "They shall be given into his hand for a time, two times, and half a time." This corresponds to 8:14, "For two thousand and three hundred evenings and mornings," and 12:11, "a thousand two hundred and ninety days," and 12:12, "a thousand three hundred and thirty-five days." In any case the seer does not expect the Maccabees to bring about the turning point of history; at best they can offer only "a little help" (11:34). True deliverance will come from above. The purpose of the visions and the legends is to encourage the people to hold on until that time comes.

Only in connection with the visions can we speak of "apocalyptic," a means of unveiling the future. Apocalyptic literature had its forerunners in Isaiah 24–27, Ezekiel 38–39, Joel, and Zechariah 12–14, but it is primarily in the next period of Judaism that it plays a significant role, and it is indispensable for an understanding of the New Testament. Scholars are agreed only on the outlines of what is typical of apocalyptic. The writers always used pseudonyms. They pointed to wise men and seers of the distant past, and their vision spans the entire cosmos and the whole of history from creation to the beginning of the eschatological kingdom of God (Dan. 7:2 f., 27). The most recent phase of history, that in which the author is living, is described more in detail, but even everything that precedes it is to be understood as prophecy. Since it has been fulfilled, it gives the seer's message a legitimacy and strengthens belief in the ultimate turning point. The difference between apocalyptic and classical prophecy is to be seen not only in the fact that the writers are pseudonymous and that the content spans world history, but primarily in the complete contrast between two ages, the present evil age which has long been developing as such and is now almost unbearable, and the coming new age of the kingdom of God. The most famous example in the Book of Daniel is found in chapter 7, where the "son of man" comes on the clouds of heaven. God gives him all power, and his dominion is without end (7:13–14). He is quite distinct from the Messiah of the prophets, who is a descendant of the family of David (Isa. 11; Mic. 5). The New Testament understood Jesus in terms of this "son of man," because in him we can see the approach of the transformation at the end of time. The New Testament then continues an interpretation of the prophetic writings which was characteristic in some respects of the apocalyptic literature. On the basis of the new factors it discovers in the old texts a second meaning. Thus in Daniel 9, the seventy years during which, according to Jeremiah's prophecy (Jer. 25:11 f.; 29:10), Jerusalem was to lie in ruins, have become seventy weeks of years (compare Dan. 9:2 with 9:24), that is, four hundred ninety years. In this way, a text from the sixth century and the current situation of the second century were brought into a relationship in which one helped to interpret the other. One of the most vexed questions of contemporary research is whether such apocalyptic is to be understood more in the light of wisdom literature or of prophetic proclamation.

EXCURSUS: *Major Problems of Old Testament Studies*

This is a good point at which to examine a few of the major problems of Old Testament studies. These problems arise to a large extent from texts discovered in the Middle East. Between

1929 and 1939, and again after the Second World War, French excavations at Ras Shamra on the northern coast of Syria, across from the eastern tip of Cyprus, uncovered a wealth of texts from the ancient royal city of Ugarit. These texts date mainly from the Late Bronze Age, that is, the centuries immediately before Israel settled in Palestine. They were written in the oldest alphabetic script in the world, in an old Canaanite dialect that has provided large amounts of material for Hebrew philology. The cultic-mythological texts enable us to determine more precisely than before what the relationship of the belief in Yahweh is to its environment. Since 1933 the French have also excavated at Tell Hariri on the central Euphrates, bringing to light the ancient city of Mari, with its royal archives dating from the eighteenth century B.C. These clay tablets provide, for example, typical names and travel routes that serve as a basis of comparison with the period of the patriarchs, as well as extensive correspondence that casts light on the question of the prehistory of Old Testament prophecy in Mesopotamia. In the caves at Khirbet Qumran on the northwest shore of the Dead Sea there were discovered beginning in 1947 a number of complete texts of Old Testament books and many fragmentary ones dating from the second century B.C., which cast considerable light on the transmission of the original text of the Bible. In addition there are commentaries on the biblical writings, a number of psalms, and other writings of the community that had its center there (e.g., the so-called Sectarian Document). These Dead Sea Scrolls enable us to see the methods of exposition of the Old Testament in the period between the two Testaments and a strand of Jewish eschatological piety of that time.

The most significant problems that scholars confront are provided by the texts of the Old Testament itself. For the early history of Israel two problems continue to claim major attention, because of the difficulty of interpreting the traditional material.

They are the figure of Moses and the forms of the organization of Israel in the period before the formation of the Israelite state. Moreover, the prehistory of the prophetic writings within Israel has not by any means been adequately explained. Studies of the transmission and editing of the materials orally and in writing keep alive the question of the existence of schools of wisdom learning, cultic schools, and schools at the royal court. Electronic data processing has been attempted in the area of statistics on words and forms.

The confrontation of Old Testament studies with systematic theology and the life of the church is neglected at present. How does the question of God today relate to the Old Testament distinction between Yahweh and the gods? What gives legitimacy to our talk about God? What is the significance of the people of God for the world of the nations? Do God's acts, to which Scripture bears witness, determine the actions of men, as the fear of God was determinative for wisdom literature and general human knowledge? How can such major problems of the Old Testament serve as a corrective for our contemporary questions? In what way can knowledge of Old Testament literary and speech forms lead us to a renewal of contemporary proclamation?

OLD AND NEW: THE RELATIONSHIP OF THE TWO TESTAMENTS

What does the Old Testament have to say to our age? Ever since this question was raised in such a pointed manner in the New Testament each generation has had to ask it anew for itself. The question cannot be properly answered, however, unless the reader first notes how the various writings and strands of the Old Testament themselves handle the matter of the relationship between old and new.

The question is not as simple as many people today think. The Old Testament reminds us of the truth of the statement, "There is nothing new under the sun" (Eccles. 1:9). It is no accident that this insight is part of that "wisdom" about life which Israel shared to such a large extent with the surrounding countries. It gave expression to the experience that in wide areas of life each generation can only repeat the insights of the previous one—truths about birth and death, sleeping and waking, keeping silent and speaking are valid everywhere and in every age. In such areas the new resembles the old, and it is the part of wisdom to regard the old as valid. To the extent that this type of wisdom is found in the Old Testament as well as in the New, every person of understanding accepts it as willingly as he does the wisdom of all the nations of the world.

This is true, however, of only limited portions of the Bible. As far as the more extensive historical and prophetic materials are concerned the heart of the Bible is to be seen rather in the distinction between the old and the new. The historical works provide a number of illustrations. After the flood, mankind lived under very different conditions from those before the flood. The unity of mankind is irretrievably lost when the languages become mutually unintelligible. Through God's call to Israel's ancestors the opportunity was opened for the races of the earth that were under the curse to receive life and blessing. For the Yahwist, each phase of history brought something new under the sun. The patriarchs increase and become a great nation; the nation is rescued from Egypt and led through the wilderness into the promised land. Had any of this ever happened before? In the Deuteronomic writings too Yahweh is the God who brings the great crises of history which produce situations that had never existed before. We see this in the transition from the leadership of Moses and Joshua to the time of the judges, then to the time of the monarchy, and finally to the time of exile. The course of history is irreversible. The old must give way to the new. So it is the Old Testament itself, with its demand for a historical way of thinking, that compels us to weigh the significance of the old in a new age.

The prophets sharpened this problem by putting the new that they were announcing into direct contrast with the old. It began with Amos's message about the end of the northern kingdom of Israel. From the time of Jeremiah on we find the "new" as a concept, one that was expressed in greater and greater contrast to the old (see above, pp. 95 f.). The new covenant will not be like the old one. The question of the relevance of the old seems to be decided in the negative when Second Isaiah calls out in the name of his God: "Remember not the former things, nor consider the things of old. Behold, I am doing a new thing; now it springs forth, do you not perceive it? I will make a way in the wilderness and rivers in the desert" (Isa. 43:18–19). Here the Old Testament seems to call itself in question. In the apocalyptic writings we see the contrast between the present world kingdom and the coming kingdom of God drawn most sharply (see above, pp. 136 f.). Certainly it is the Old Testament itself that leads us to the sharp distinction, indeed to a view of the old age and the new as irreconcilably opposed. Anyone who is inclined to a radical rethinking of the problem of the Old Testament in a new era must rethink it in terms of the Old Testament itself.

This then points up the real contrast to what is new. The old is gone. And wherever people have not been willing to let it go it has caused serious damage. The accounts of the wars in the days of the judges and the kings have been used to justify the cruelty of "Christian" military campaigns. The setting apart of Israel from among the nations has been made to serve as surety for nationalistic and religious pharisaism. Priestly legal ordinances have been called on to legitimate hierarchical structures and cultic ideas of sacrifice. In every case what was involved was the kind of unhistorical thinking that the Old Testament itself had overcome. That was what produced such devastation in Christian faith and life. It was a matter not only of falling below the teachings of the New Testament but also of ignoring the guidance provided by the Old Testament for distinguishing between old and new. What then is the purpose of all those stories and laws? They serve first of all to keep us aware of the contrast between what Jesus of Nazareth brought into history and everything that is contrary to him in what went before. Paul tells us that many things that happened in the Old Testament were "written down for our instruction" (1 Cor. 10:11); they open the eyes of contemporary readers for things that ought to belong to the past as things that have been overcome. Let me mention two examples of things that the crucifixion of Jesus relegated to what is old.

The Priestly Document formulated capital punishment as an ordinance for mankind after the flood, in order to provide unconditional protection for human life in contrast to the life of animals. "Whoever sheds the blood of man, by man shall his blood be shed" (Gen. 9:6; cf. 9:2). This means of protecting human life should now lie behind us, because all four Gospels in parallel passages place in connection with the execution of Jesus the amnesty for a notorious man who had perhaps even committed murder in his revolutionary activities, and who had in any case been sentenced to death (Matt. 27:16 f., 21 f.; Mark 15:7, 11; Luke 23:18; John 18:40).

As a second example of things that have been superseded, I want to mention certain mythological ways of talking about God that have been introduced into theological thought. According to the synoptic Gospels the prayer in Psalm 22, "My God, my God, why hast thou forsaken me?" is a part of the death of

Christ. God is here documented as the one totally concealed. At Easter the one whom God had abandoned shows himself to the discouraged disciples as the true witness to the living God. Since then, God is not found any longer taking a stroll in the cool of the evening, or in a dream at the top of a ladder leading to heaven, or in the storm of questions that burst over Job out of the whirlwind. Rather, as the living God, he is to be sought in this Jesus who was forsaken and then raised from the dead, and in the message of freedom that points to him.

And yet the direction that leads to God is to be found already in the midst of the old. There is such a thing as falling below what is old into what is even older. In Deuteronomy there is a law that provides that a disobedient son who cannot be handled by his parents should be taken before the elders of the city. Although stress is not laid on this, the son is thereby in fact removed from arbitrary or unfair action on the part of his parents (Deut. 21:18–21; cf. 25:1–3). Even Cain, who murdered his brother, is protected against blood revenge by the word of Yahweh and by the mark that is placed on him (Gen. 4:15). Those who in the Psalms prayed for revenge did not themselves act to secure it, but left the judgment to the hidden God (see above, p. 109). Even in cases of this sort, of course, there is something old that should not be revived. A historical view of things suggests that we today should beware of falling below the level of the Old Testament documents. This gives to the Old Testament, as compared with the New, the function of a historical mirror in which we are to examine our consciences. But to admit this function is to grasp only a part of the significance of the Old Testament for an understanding of the New.

The Old Testament also makes clear the basis of the New. If we look only at the two examples given above as helps in understanding Jesus' death on the cross, its full meaning can be seen only by listening to the prophetic words that point beyond themselves. The effort to liberate a mankind worthy of death is seen as a matter of God's will. As such, it has had a long previous history. If we fail to take this into account we will never be able to grasp the historical event of the execution of Jesus as the goal and seal of God's will. We are to understand the mark that protected Cain, the other instances in which the Yahwist testifies to God's patience with those who are under a curse, and God's intention of blessing all nations on earth as pointing in this direction. Hosea's message about God's passionate, unconditional love for an incorrigible Israel that has corrupted every relationship of life and love (see above, pp. 92 f.) becomes a means to help us understand the cross as the action in which God reveals himself. Second Isaiah leads us to understand events of history in terms of the prior prophetic word as God's actions (see above, p. 98). The case is similar with respect to the dying Jesus' abandonment by God, which is illumined by the quoting of Psalm 22. In the early documents of Israel's history, as well as in prophecy, we found that the concealment of God was steadily increasing. According to Isa. 45:14 f. God, as the Savior, completely conceals himself in the history of Israel. According to Second Isaiah's promise the nations are to discover this. This then shows the amazing road from mythological descriptions of God to the theology of the cross. I have no idea how anyone who fails to take this road into account can expect to discover in the cross of Jesus the origin of a movement of total freedom and at the same time the place where the hidden God reveals himself. The rejection of the Old Testament and of Easter go hand in hand (Luke 16:31). We would not be keeping pace with the New Testament witnesses if we did not include among our modern sources of knowledge the Old Testament, for it is the key to an understanding of the story of

Jesus. The Old Testament has been superseded not primarily as something that is past but as something that has been fulfilled in the New. This involves much more than merely regarding it as the basis for the New.

The Old Testament also casts light on the goal of the New Testament. It makes announcement of that which has still not been achieved today. We should think in this connection of those amazing Old Testament prophecies which found a certain embodiment in Jesus but which have still not been realized in the world of contemporary history. They constitute that aspect of the Old Testament which goes beyond even the story of Jesus and stimulates the New Testament community to lively expectation. The goal will be reached only when sorrow and death, which were conquered in the life of Jesus, are seen by all to have been finally ended in a new heaven and a new earth (cf. Isa. 65:17; 66:22; Rev. 21:1 ff.).

The promises of the Old Testament give its readers ultimate goals, which serve a dual function throughout the New Testament. First, in the confusion of current circumstances they point the way to final things, and second, in the midst of the depressingly slow progress of history they awaken the power to look for those things on which we can rely. An important function of the Old Testament is to keep our attention fixed on the goal of the New Testament, so that we do not regard any of the blind alleys and muddy lanes of contemporary life as having final validity.

But how is it possible for the present generation, given the great diversity of Old Testament expectations, to keep clearly in view this goal of the New Testament? Isn't it possible in the chaos of the Old Testament texts for each person to find whatever he wants? This is where the task of critical understanding begins.

EXCURSUS: *Principles of Interpretation*

see Canon & Authority
p 112

One of the first principles of understanding the Bible is that we must identify the persons to whom the ancient witness was addressing his message. We must then leave it to the text to seek out in the present day the reader who corresponds to the one to whom it was originally addressed. But is it possible for anyone today to correspond to the original recipients of the message? Isn't this type of analogical thinking unhistorical? It would be folly to deny the value of analogies. Anyone who rejects the analogies that accompany history is blind to the recurrence of similar dangers, temptations, and plights. It is well here to remember the truth of the insights of wisdom literature (see above, p. 140). To be sure, the historical differences must be included in the process by which we seek to understand the message. They are to be noted more in the situation of the messengers than in that of their hearers. In terms of the goal, the most important differences are to be found in the words of Jesus and in the fate that befell him. We must distinguish between goals that the New Testament left behind and those that it took up and gave new power and expectation. The Old Testament hope must pass through the fire of New Testament criticism. But in the same way the Old Testament promises bring to bear a critique that protects the word of the New Testament from misunderstandings. The self-evident biblical presuppositions of the documents of the early church can be misunderstood as setting goals only for individuals, and only spiritual or exclusively otherworldly goals at that. So the constant comparison of the two Testaments with each other enables us to understand them both better.

Three areas of promise may be mentioned which we can expect will find attentive students in this present age that is so lacking in goals. The first is fully stated by the Yahwist in the motto, "In you all the families of the earth shall be blessed" (Gen. 12:3). Its purpose is to open the eyes of a church that is all too concerned with itself and show it God's final purpose, where mankind is seen as a unit and help is to be given to all. Paul connects this hope to Christ (Gal. 3:8) and so gives it new power. The message of Isa. 19:23–25 is a stimulus to understanding the word in concrete terms: "In that day Israel will be the third with Egypt and Assyria, a blessing in the midst of the earth," Assyria and Egypt representing the two great power blocks which stood over against one another in the world of the ancient Near East. Hence this unusual word leads to a second area of promise, peace among all the nations. According to Isa. 2:2–4 the teachings of Zion's God will in the end bring about the transformation of all weapons of war into implements of peace. With many variations the message is brought home to a people suffering violence, telling them that they must not abandon hope in the one who will bring in an era of endless peace, based on right and justice (Mic. 5:3 f.; Isa. 9:5 f.; Zech. 9:9 f.). Ezekiel combined this second area of promise, the life of freedom, with a third, the goal of knowing God: "I will make with them a covenant of peace. . . . and they shall know that I am the Lord, when I break the bars of their yoke, and deliver them from the hand of those who enslave them" (Ezek. 34:25– 27). In our present life we have at best a fragmentary knowledge of God, preserved by the authority of individuals and passed on by teachers. At our goal, however, we will all gain full, direct knowledge (Jer. 31:34). Both young and old, men and women, slaves and free will have it (Joel 3:1 f.). The psalms of the kingship of Yahweh are anticipations of the jubilation that will break out over such a fullness of life for everyone—life with peace and a knowledge of God that is no longer fragmentary. "The princes of the peoples gather as the people of the God of Abraham" (Ps. 47:9*a*) Thus the transcendent promises of the Old Testament express the goal of the New in clear and concrete terms that cast their brilliant light on the present in which we live.

Most Old Testament texts point the way from the Old to the New. Because they still have not attained to what is new, but are only moving toward it, they serve as helps for all later generations, which, in the midst of transitory things, are searching for the way that leads to things of lasting validity. Without the Old Testament, the New cannot be the Bible which men need today as a companion in the midst of our troubles in this present world.

Conclusion: The Old Testament in Theology, Church, and Society

Theology must never relinquish the theme of the Old Testament. Indeed it must see to it that in each generation the Old Testament becomes once again a theme of theology. The texts of the Old Testament again and again provide theology with that knowledge of God which it needs—and which it is possible to have, albeit in fragmentary form. In a world that has been emptied of gods, the distinction between Yahweh and the gods prevents theology from paying homage either to religious propositions that are supposed to be self-evident, or to atheistic platitudes. Job and Ecclesiastes force theology to remember its hard-pressed contemporaries. Karl Barth reminds us that the New Testament is hidden in the Old, and the Old unfolds in the New. He continues: "Theology has always faced the danger of shriveling up if it neglected this insight, or if it attempted to exist in a vacuum, oriented only to the New Testament."

Where theology does not forsake this given theme, it will also be able to provide a critical service to the church. It will remind the church of the danger of imitating Jonah, who wanted to reserve God's compassion for himself alone. God

149

used Jonah even though he was more obstinate than the heathen. If the Book of Jonah rescues the Christian church from its narrow expectations, the Psalms can bring the church to sing the praise of God and his mercy as the basic note of all its pronouncements and as the motivating force of all its activities. The church will then not regard its provisional work for a rebellious and troubled mankind as hopeless.

The Old Testament points the church more toward everyday life than toward the Sunday community. Its promises keep the church from pursuing lesser goals, from giving up the task altogether, or from trying to do the job on its own as a shortcut. The Old Testament is oriented toward this world. It helps keep the focus on doing what is within the realm of possibility. We have to learn to live with that. This book is intended as a help in that direction. It leaves its readers to apply to the Old Testament the question asked by Georg Christoph Lichtenberg: "If a book and a head collide and there is a hollow sound, is it all the book's fault?" The Bible can wait.

It is waiting.

Indexes

NAMES AND SUBJECTS

151

SCRIPTURE REFERENCES